Copyright © Matt Bennett 2023

All rights reserved. No part of this publication may be reproduced, distributed, or transmitted in any form or by any means, including photocopying, recording, or other electronic or mechanical methods, without the prior written permission of the author, except in the case of brief quotations embodied in critical reviews and certain other noncommercial uses permitted by copyright law. For permission requests, write to the publisher, addressed "Attention: Permissions Coordinator," at the address below.

Published by: Matt Bennett May 2023

Matt@Myrawintuition.com www.Myrawintuition.com

DISCLAIMER

The information and recipes contained within this book are neither intended to treat, cure, or diagnose any disease or illness, nor meant to replace your healthcare professional or family physician's advice. The techniques and advice described in this book represent the opinions of the author based on his experience. The author expressly disclaims any responsibility for any liability, loss or risk, personal or otherwise, which is incurred as a result of using any of the techniques, recipes, or recommendations suggested herein. If in any doubt, or if requiring medical advice, please contact the appropriate health professional.

Table of Contents

Introduction..1
   The Great Deficiency..............................1
   Falling For Euphemisms 5
   Break Free From The Industry Spell............5
   The Modern Frugivore............................10
   Redefining The Main Course...................12
1. The Most Neglected Superfood In
   The Human Diet...................................16
      A True Superfood.............................16
         Popeye Had It Right....................17
         Green Protein............................18
         Calcium....................................19
         Iron..20
         Magnesium...............................20
         Vitamin C..................................21
         Folate (Vitamin B9).....................21
         Vitamin K..................................22
         Omega-3s.................................23
         Nitrates....................................24
         Prebiotic Fibers.........................24
         Chlorophyll...............................25
         Detoxification Support................26
         Cognitive Function.....................27
         Weight Optimization..................28
2. Greens In Abundance...........................31
      Wild Edibles...................................35
      Indoor and Outdoor Gardening............36
         Outdoor Gardens......................36
         Potted Herbs............................37
         Microgreens.............................39

  Sprouts..42
  Domestic Diversity vs Natural Abundance.....45
  The Sad American Diet.......................... 48
  Fresh is Best....................................49
  Plants Educate the Body........................ 50
3. Clean Greens...................................... 51
  What's The Problem With Pesticides............52
    Non-monotonic Dose Responses........ 55
    The Cocktail Effect: 1 + 1 = 2000...... 56
  Toxicity Beyond Pesticides....................... 57
    Sewage Sludge........................... 57
4. Green Myths....................................... 60
  Alkaloids..61
  Oxalates.. 63
  Goitrogens...................................... 67
  Halogens.. 69
    Bromine................................. 70
    Chlorine................................ 72
    Fluoride................................ 74
  Bacterial Contamination......................... 77
  Anti-nutrients...................................79
    Anti-nutrients Are Hormetic..............80
    Anti-nutrients Are Nutrients.............81
5. The Proof Is In The Salad Bowl.....................83
  My Green Team....................................84
    Tanny Raw............................... 84
    Dan McDonald............................ 85
    John Kohler............................. 87
    Dr. Fred Bisci.......................... 88
    Dr. Caldwell Esselstyn.................. 90
    Dr. T. Colin Campbell....................92
    Dr. Ann Wigmore......................... 94
6. Stumbling Over Salads..............................97

Why People Struggle To Eat Greens............97
Common Salad Mistakes To Avoid..............100
    Too Few Calories.......................... 100
    Poorly Prepared Ingredients..............102
    Inadequate Equipment.................... 104
    Not Enough Variety.......................107
    Too Much Fat............................ 109
    The Wrong Mindset...................... 110
Building Your Green Esteem.....................113
    Green Smoothies..........................114
    Green Juices............................. 116
    Find Your Green Team..................... 119

7. The New Main Course............................ 121
The Science of Salads............................ 122
    Structure.................................. 123
        What Does One Pound of
        Greens Look Like?..................126
    Sense-appeal............................. 128
        Appearance.......................... 128
        Smell................................ 129
        Feel.................................. 130
        Taste................................ 131
        Hitting Your Bliss Points........... 133
    Satiation................................. 133
        Stretch Receptors...................134
        Nutrient Sensors....................134
        Calorie Sensors..................... 135
Every Main Course Needs An Appetizer........ 138
Consciously Cooked Additions Are Optional.. 138
Designing Your Shopping List.................... 140
    Staple Items To Have On Hand.......... 140
    Buying Your Greens...................... 141
    Buying Your Vegetables....................142

    Buying Your Fruits............................ 143
    Time-Saving Tips................................. 145
    Recommended Products and Tools.............. 147
    Follow The Salad Science........................152
8. Welcome To The Revolution........................ 154
    Join the 5-Star Salad Self-Report Study........ 155
9. Recipes... 157
    Green Smoothies................................... 157
        Blue Collard.................................157
        Kale Berry................................... 158
        Green Gulp................................... 158
        Bok On The Beach......................... 158
        Kale Basil Blast............................159
        Chocolate Shake........................... 159
        Romaine Empire........................... 159
        Pear Zinger.................................. 160
        Pear-A-Dice................................. 160
        Berry Mango Glory........................ 160
    Green Juices...................................... 161
        True Green.................................. 162
        Ginger Romaine............................ 161
        Purple Potion............................... 161
        Liver Massage.............................. 162
        Pineapple Mint Tonic..................... 162
        Fennel Therapy.............................162
        I'll Be Bok................................... 163
        Dill and Chill............................... 163
        Green Earth................................. 163
        Tangelo Twister........................... 163
    Salad Dressings...................................164
        Macarena.................................... 164
        Onion and Chive.......................... 164
        Creamy Oregano........................... 165

Smokey Chive.................................165
Cranberry Anise............................ 166
Purple Haze.................................. 166
Pickle Spice................................... 166
Macadamia Fire............................ 167
Macadill Ranch..............................167
Cuminator.....................................168
Fentastic...................................... 168
Brazilian Heat.............................. 169
Cajun Mango................................ 169
Mango Thyme.............................. 170
Mango Red.................................. 170
Southwest Chipotle....................... 171
Sesame Nori................................. 171

Fat-Free Salad Dressings......................... 172
Frawnch...................................... 172
Honey-Less Mustard..................... 172
Apricot Infusion........................... 172
Purple Surge................................ 173
Black Magic................................. 173

5-Star Salads.. 174
Cajun Berry Mango 5-Star Salad........ 175
Citrus Herb 5-Star Salad.................. 176
Apple Cranberry 5-Star Salad............ 177
Cumin Get It 5-Star Salad.................178
Pineapple Raspberry 5-Star Salad...... 179
Basil Mango Thyme 5-Star Salad........ 180
Pineapple Ranch 5-Star Salad............181
Cranberry Macarena 5-Star Salad....... 182
Spicy Mango Red 5-Star Salad........... 183
Macadamia Fire 5-Star Salad............ 184
Apple Berry 5-Star Salad.................. 185
Fentastic 5-Star Salad......................186

Southwest Chipotle 5-Star Salad........	187
In A Pickle 5-Star Salad...................	188
10. Green Wisdom...	189
About The Author...	201
Other Paperback Books By Matt Bennett...........	202
Acknowledgments..	203

Introduction

We need a shift in the collective mindset from "meat and potatoes" to "greens and tomatoes." - Matt Bennett

The Great Deficiency

If I told you that around 97% of Americans were deficient in an essential nutrient, would you believe me? Could this be? Wouldn't this be headline news? Not so much.

The truth is, this great deficiency does exist, but you won't see it listed on your blood work. This seemingly elusive nutrient is hiding in the garnish that often gets pushed to the side of the plate and later into the trash. Trace amounts can be found tucked between the white flour bun and the beef burger that many Americans eat on a regular basis.

The essential nutrient that I'm talking about is fiber, and its shortage in the American diet should be a major cause for concern. A lack of dietary fiber is linked to many chronic diseases, including heart disease, diabetes, gut dysbiosis, dementia, and cancer.

Fiber is a special type of complex carbohydrate found in plants. It is not broken down by our digestive enzymes but instead consumed by beneficial bacteria as it travels through the intestines, imparting numerous important benefits to human health.

Without a consistent supply of fiber, these essential gut bacteria cannot survive and this gives way to various pathogenic microbes that can cause damage to the gut lining and lead to numerous chronic health problems throughout the body.

Only about 3% of Americans are consuming the USDA minimum recommended daily value of dietary fiber intake. That's bananas! It is recommended that adult women get at least 28 grams, and adult men get 34 grams of fiber each day. That may sound like a lot, but even those recommendations are setting a low standard, considering indigenous groups, like the Hadza of Tanzania, reportedly consume more than 100 grams of fiber daily.

With that said, I do not recommend that you immediately aim to eat 100 grams of fiber in one day if your current average intake is closer to 10 or 15 grams.

As Dr. Will Bulsiewicz, MD, author of *Fiber Fueled,* says, "Think of the gut like a muscle" that we must gradually increase its fiber workload over time to avoid injury, or in this case - serious digestive discomfort.

You wouldn't go to the gym for the first time and instantly pick up the heaviest weights. You would start out with a manageable amount of lighter weight and over the course of several weeks or months, increase the weight as your muscles become stronger.

Sticking with the gym analogy, you also would not want to do the same exercise every time you go to the gym - you get the best results when you incorporate a wide variety of exercises. This is also true for the gut - increasing slowly over time and eating a relatively wide variety of plant foods will provide the strongest, most robust gut.

Unfortunately, what we are seeing today are the consequences of the hyper-stimulating, fiber-deficient, Westernized diets, and medicated lifestyles that have left so many people's "gut muscles" weak, leaky, and inflamed.

The gut is the centerpiece of the body and is responsible for absorbing the vital nutrition we need to live while at the same time, preventing harmful pathogens from getting into the body. If the gut becomes weak, every aspect of the body and mind is at an increased risk of becoming compromised. So, it is no surprise that in today's populations, we are seeing epidemic levels of chronic physical and mental diseases throughout every age group.

The solution is to drastically change how we eat, live, and think. We must acknowledge the great deficiency that is at the core of our collective health adversities. We must no longer accept living with weak and sluggish digestion, perpetually widening waste lines, or feelings of fear and helplessness with regard to our health and happiness.

What I have found is that our diet can be a powerful catalyst to unlocking the more expansive parts of the mind, and allowing for a wider scope of awareness and appreciation for life - or it can push us further into fear and self-sabotage - depending on what we choose to eat.

When we bring more of God's frequency into our bodies through fresh fruits and vegetables, our level of consciousness, creativity, and compassion increase exponentially. We begin to see new possibilities and meaning in ourselves and everything around us as we more easily tap into a growth-oriented mindset.

Thankfully, every year more people are becoming aware of the incredible life transformations that are possible with a plant-based diet. However, with this ever-increasing interest in plant-based diets, the fake-food industry has responded with more and more processed plant-based products to take advantage of the growing market. Because of this, it is now possible to eat a plant-based diet without ever eating any actual plants!

Instead of fresh fruits and vegetables, many people are led astray by plant-based chicken nuggets, sausage links, egg substitutes, pizza, burgers, hot dogs, etc. While these items do not contain animal products, they are still calorie-rich and full of processed sugars, oils, salt, synthetic chemical flavorings, preservatives, low amounts of fiber, and little to no hydration.

The familiarity that people have with these food-like products makes them very attractive to those who are transitioning away from animal products. Amongst all of the unknowns and challenges of changing such a big part of one's lifestyle, it makes people feel comfortable and safe when they can eat something that looks, tastes and feels familiar. They see it as a win-win. However, these wins are short-lived.

While it is great to see more people choosing plant-based options, the fact is that processed foods - plant-based or not - will never provide the level of health and vitality that most people expect when they switch to a plant-based diet.

Falling For Euphemisms

The meat, dairy, and processed food industries have successfully taken advantage of euphemisms from day one. Hamburgers, hot dogs, chicken nuggets, steak, etc., are labels that are used to avoid verbalizing that these are pieces of dead animal body parts - to put it lightly. Just as donuts, cake, cookies, and candy, are words we used to distract people from the fact that they are eating a conglomeration of synthetic chemicals, refined flour, sugars, oils, and salt. If we applied accurate descriptions to many of the products that people consume, there would be a lot more critical thinking being done when it comes to people's diets.

Looking beyond the label is an important principle that every consumer should follow as closely as possible. Before buying any food or product with an ingredient list, make it an automatic habit to review the listed ingredients and verify that you are comfortable allowing them in your body. Understanding how to interpret labels and researching the ingredients in the products you buy will help you avoid falling victim to industry euphemisms, deceptive labeling, and other advertising tactics.

It is time that we awaken from the spell that has deceived us into seeing packaged products as food. We must open our eyes and clearly see these products for what they are - toxic obstructions to our vitality.

Break Free From The Industry Spell

I too was once under the illusion that processed foods and animal products were healthy forms of nourishment for the human body. Whether it came from a box, carton, or even a drive-through window - if it was high in protein or calcium, it had to be good for me.

I also understood that fruits and vegetables were healthy, but in my mind, those were secondary foods. After all, I never once saw a TV commercial tell me how important it was to eat fruits or vegetables unless they were flavoring for my yogurt or breakfast cereal! So how important could fruits and vegetables really be!? I would soon find out.

For virtually my entire childhood, I suffered from frequent illnesses, including asthma, eczema, dry skin, ear infections, sore throats, allergies, insomnia, colds, and flu. I never for a second thought that my diet and lifestyle could be causing any of these issues. I just knew that there was a pink or blue medicine for each of these problems that I could take to make it go away - and that was good enough for me!

However, when I started losing my hair at sixteen, I couldn't find an effective medicine to make that go away, though I tried. Finding a solution to hair loss completely consumed my mind and psychologically affected every aspect of my life. I tried creams, pills, gels, shampoos, concealers, homemade DIY potions, headstands, scalp massages, visualization meditations, eating extra protein, supplements, and even a transplant surgery - nothing worked.

A significant change I made at the age of 21 was adding an abundance of leafy greens to my diet. During my prolific experimentation and research into the prevention of hair loss, I learned that leafy greens are an excellent source of protein, vitamins, and minerals known to promote healthy hair. So, three to five nights a week I was eating a giant leafy green salad full of colorful vegetables, fresh garlic, garbanzo beans, chicken flesh, shredded cheese, and ranch dressing. Certainly not my proudest salad creation, but it was an important first step to move me in the direction of where I am today.

Three years later I heard about the benefits of drinking freshly pressed fruit and vegetable juices. Somehow I knew I needed to give juicing a try - probably because I had tried everything else! So, I started with the intention of doing a three-day juice fast, but by the third day, I was feeling so good that I decided to keep going!

It wasn't until the tenth day that I decided to break my fast and the results were nothing short of amazing. My skin was clearer, I was breathing easier, my sleep was better, my toxic thinking had greatly improved, I had amazing energy, I was less constipated, and I lost some of the fat around my waist.

My entire worldview was turned upside down. I had just consumed nothing but the juices of what I thought were secondary foods (fruits and vegetables) in the absence of my prized animal protein. How could I feel this good? I set out on a mission to make sense of what I was experiencing.

The more I researched and the more fresh fruits and vegetables I consumed, the further I was being pulled from the illusions that had clouded my perceptions around health and my self-image. Suddenly, my focus began shifting away from an obsession over my hair and physical body, and more towards appreciating who I was and growing spiritually. The industry spell had been lifted from my mind and I was seeing myself and the world from a fresh new lens!

My insatiable desire to learn more led me to the teachings of Dr. Robert Morse, N.D., who helped to further clarify what I was experiencing. He explained that every animal in nature has a species-specific diet, which was perfectly suited for their biological design. He went on to describe the four classifications of vertebrates:

Carnivore
Includes: Cats, lions, tigers, etc.
Diet: Meats, some vegetables, grass, herbs
Digestive System: Large mouth opening, unidirectional jaw (up and down only), large canine teeth, rough tongue, less than or equal to 1 pH with food in the stomach, smooth and short small intestine – 3 to 6 times body length, short and smooth non-sacculated colon
Extremities: Claws on hands and feet, quadrupeds (walk on all fours)

Omnivore
Includes: Dogs, hogs, chickens, bears, etc.
Diet: Meat, vegetables, fruits, roots
Digestive System: Large mouth opening, multi-directional jaw, sharp canine teeth or beaks, moderate to rough tongue, less than or equal to 1 pH with food in the stomach, somewhat sacculated small intestine – 4 to 6 times body length, short and smooth colon
Extremities: Hoofs, claws, and paws, quadrupeds (walk on all fours) – except birds.

Herbivore
Includes: Horses, cows, elephants, giraffes, etc.
Diet: Vegetables, grasses, herbs, roots, barks
Digestive System: Small mouth opening, multi-directional jaw, broad and flat molars made for grinding – small or no canines, moderately rough tongue, 4 to 5 pH with food in the stomach, long and sacculated small intestine – 10 to 12+ times body length, long and sacculated colon
Extremities: hoofs, quadrupeds (walk on all fours)

Frugivore
Includes: Bonobos, Gorillas, Chimpanzees, etc.
Diet: Mainly fruits, leafy greens, vegetables, nuts, seeds
Digestive System: Small mouth opening, multi-directional

jaw, usually 32 teeth (including incisors, canines – short and blunted, premolars, and molars), smooth tongue, 4 to 5 pH with food in the stomach, long and sacculated small intestine – 10 to 11 times body length, long and sacculated colon
Extremities: Hands with fingers, feet with toes, capable of bipedalism (uses two legs for walking - walks upright)

I had never heard it broken down in this way before, but once I did, it made so much sense. It was becoming clear why I felt such a shift in my body, mind, and spirit. I could see there is only one group of vertebrates that the human species fits into perfectly – Frugivore!

To be clear - being a frugivore, as indicated above, does not mean that we are meant to only eat fruit – but that we would generally prefer fruit over other options when available. Every species on Earth seeks the food that its body is physiologically designed to digest, absorb, utilize, and eliminate the most efficiently – nature always seeks efficiency. For humans, that food is fruit, as it takes minimal effort for the body to break it down and utilize its energy.

Fruit is full of simple sugars, vitamins, minerals, antioxidants, polyphenols, hydration, prebiotic fiber, and other phytochemicals that help to power our brain and nervous system. Our color vision helps us spot a ripe apple, mango, or strawberry while out in nature. Our sense of smell is calibrated to the tantalizing fragrances of fruits and berries. Our hands are perfectly formed to pluck fruits from a tree, and our fingers to peel them. And we have a smooth tongue that is designed to enjoy the sweet flavors of fruits (and vegetables).

In regards to eating animals, we are disgusted by the sight and smell of a bloody carcass and deeply disturbed by the sound of an animal in pain. Have you ever lost your appetite after finding a random hair in your meal? These sorts of things would not deter an animal that was meant to eat the flesh of other animals.

The Modern Frugivore

There are some who believe humans are a pure fruitarian species that thrive eating only fruit. Through my research, observation, and personal experience, I do not believe this to be the case - at least not for the modern frugivore.

Perhaps this is possible for those that live in the tropics and have access to perfectly tree-ripened fruits grown in rich, healthy soils. Though, even in that case, I'm not sure it would be optimal.

Our closest primate relatives, chimpanzees, and bonobos eat a significant amount of leafy greens and other items in their diet. While fruit is their favorite food, they also eat more than 113 types of plants, including leaves, flowers, seeds, bark, fungus, and honey. They may also eat insects and occasionally small mammals when their preferred foods are scarce, but this is for survival and makes up less than 2% of their diet.

I love fruit as much as anyone, but from the information and anecdotal cases that I have reviewed, the chances of doing well long-term on an all-fruit diet are not good. For a pure fruitarian diet to have any chance at working, I suspect it would need to be composed of high-quality, tree-ripened tropical fruits, which is not practical for the average person.

Instead, the majority of people (including myself) rely on grocery stores to supply their fruit. Store-bought fruit is almost always picked unripe to prevent bruising and spoilage during the transportation process. This also gives it a longer shelf life once it's in the store.

When fruit is picked before it reaches full maturity, it is not able to develop its full nutrient profile. This means potentially fewer vitamins, minerals, and antioxidants than it was intended to have.

Greens and vegetables don't have this problem, and they are generally richer in minerals than fruits in the first place, so they can be helpful for filling in some of the potential gaps that some store-bought fruits may have.

From my perspective, it is clear that the modern frugivore does the best on a balanced fruit, greens, and vegetable-based diet. Using fruits to provide the bulk of the calories, and leafy greens, vegetables, nuts, and seeds to optimize the mineral and micronutrient profile of the diet.

While there are basic dietary principles that I believe everyone can benefit from following (which will be discussed throughout the book), each individual needs to determine what that optimal balance will look like for them.

With that said, I believe the diets of chimps and bonobos provide a lot of useful insight into what our diet is meant to resemble - heavy on fruits and greens, with some vegetables, and a small number of nuts and seeds.

Redefining The Main Course

I wrote this book for three main reasons:

1. People don't eat nearly enough leafy greens.
2. Very few people know how to make a proper salad.
3. Nearly every person I have worked with suffers from some form of digestive problem.

This may not come as a surprise, but over the years, I have noticed whenever someone sets a goal to eat more fruits and vegetables, their struggle is rarely figuring out how to eat more fruit. The resistance comes when it is time to eat the salad!

Since I began working with people in 2016, almost invariably, I have found that people do not eat nearly enough leafy greens. And why would they, when they grew up thinking greens were just a topping to their burger and tacos?

Like me, most Americans were taught that meat is the centerpiece of the meal, potatoes or bread were the primary side dish, and maybe some canned peas or corn would make it onto your plate to add a little color. If your family was really healthy, you might have a small pinch of shredded iceberg lettuce from a bag, topped with shredded cheese and ranch dressing. Wash it all down with a glass of cow's milk, and you just had yourself a standard American meal.

When this is the reality for so many people, it is completely understandable why eating greens is such a foreign concept. Even the people who *are* eating leafy greens regularly are still severely undereating them because nobody seems to know what an appropriate amount looks like.

Due to this, you can't just ask someone if they eat a lot of greens seeing that people's perception of how they eat is rarely an accurate portrayal. It's similar to when someone says, "I eat very little meat," and then you spend a day with them and every meal has meat in it.

When I hear someone say, "Oh, I eat a lot of salad" and then I see their salad, it becomes apparent that "a lot of salad" is only a lot if you're comparing it to eating no salad.

I believe my idea of "a lot of greens" is so different from theirs because our fundamental understanding of a salad's role in the meal is at odds. They believe that salad is inherently a side dish. Whereas, I see salad as the main dish, as Dr. Joel Fuhrman would say. It just so happens that a large side dish is still smaller than a small main dish - and what I'm recommending is a large main dish!

So, what we need to do is change people's fundamental beliefs about the role greens play in our diet. At least one meal per day should consist of a large leafy green salad as the main dish. And by large, I mean *a minimum* of one pound of leafy greens. Yes, one pound! If you can make it more than that, even better! I understand that this might seem like an insurmountable goal, but I assure you that it's not nearly as difficult as it sounds - keep reading.

Over the years of hearing one person after another tell me that they struggle to eat greens because they don't enjoy salads, I started my own dietary self-assessment. I wanted to figure out how it could be that I absolutely loved my big salads and to others, "salad" was a four-letter word.

I started to study how I make my salads versus how everyone else makes theirs. The differences stood out like a sore thumb. I immediately started writing a list of all the key attributes of my salads that made them so enjoyable, and after analyzing the list, I distilled it down to five key pillars that constitute what I now call a 5-Star Salad.

I found that it was much more effective to give someone these structured guidelines to learn the basics of making a satisfying salad rather than just telling them to eat more greens. The sad reality is that very few people know the first thing about making a salad into an actual meal. With the help of this book, you will learn to create masterful 5-Star Salads and avoid the common salad-making mistakes that I see people committing every day that sabotages their salad-eating experience.

Another critical point is that the ingredients that we put into a salad are only part of why it is so enjoyable. We must also take into account what the rest of our diet is doing to our taste buds. A commonality among the people that have a hard time enjoying salads is they regularly eat processed foods. Not only does this desensitize their taste receptors, but it conditions their mind to eat for entertainment.

By eating whole, natural foods and avoiding hyper-stimulating products, I keep my tastebuds healthy and perfectly capable of finding enjoyment in the taste of nourishing leafy greens.

Additionally, my food preparation techniques are performed with the intention to optimize the mouthfeel and texture of the salad. And maybe most important is the gratitude and positive mindset that I choose to view eating delicious salads with. All of this, and more, will be covered in more detail throughout this book.

5-Star Salads have been a key factor in my success on a very high raw vegan diet over the last 12 years. These salads have not only added the perfect balance to the fruit I eat, but they have helped me to establish what I believe is a nutritionally sound way of eating that is free from cravings, binging, and the desire for "cheat days."

A daily 5-Star salad has also allowed me to create the best gut and digestive health of my life - free of constipation, foul-smelling gas, bloating, and so much more!

I used to go multiple days between bowel movements, and they were often dry and painful to pass - I dreaded going to the bathroom. Now it's an enjoyable experience with little to no smell. I guess you could say that I'm the guy who thinks his poop doesn't stink!

So, not only can 5-Star Salads help you feel nourished and satisfied, but they also support a healthy gut microbiome that will keep your digestive health running smoothly and your bathroom breaks something to look forward to!

Without further ado, let your *5-Star Salad Revolution* begin!

1

The Most Neglected Superfood In The Human Diet

A True Superfood

Leafy greens are the most neglected and under-eaten superfoods in the human diet, even among many raw food enthusiasts. Fruits understandably get much of the attention when someone is looking to include more delicious plant foods into their diet - but just as Batman needs Robin, greens play an essential role in your health-defending, superfood team.

Let's get away from the idea that superfoods come from the other side of the world and must arrive to us in fancy packages. True superfoods are whole, unprocessed plant foods" - plain and simple.

However, because much of the Westernized world has fallen under the Industry Spell and believes that factory-made, packaged products, that can sit on a shelf for several months without spoiling, are also considered "food" - we must differentiate these packaged products from the true foods - or what I label "superfoods."

Leafy greens are packed with a wide range of nutrients, including vitamins, minerals, antioxidants, chlorophyll, amino acids, and fiber. Consuming leafy greens regularly can help lower the risk of various health conditions, such as heart disease, cancer, and type 2 diabetes. They are also an excellent source of important phytonutrients, which can help improve overall health and reduce inflammation in the body.

All leafy greens are low in calories and high in fiber, making them a great option for those looking to maintain a healthy weight. When eaten in sufficient quantities, leafy greens also provide a healthy source of omega-3 fatty acids, which support a healthy brain, gut, and immune system.

There's not a cell in the body that doesn't benefit from eating more leafy greens. So, whether you add them to a salad, smoothie, juice, or stir-fry, incorporating leafy greens into your diet can help improve your overall health and well-being.

Popeye Had It Right

I remember, as a child, one of my favorite cartoons was Popeye the Sailor Man. Whenever Popeye was in trouble, he would pull out a can of spinach from his pocket, and after eating the spinach, he would instantly become stronger, faster, and more resilient.

The idea behind Popeye's love of spinach was a tribute to the real-life nutritional excellence of leafy green vegetables. The writers of this iconic cartoon clearly appreciated the multitude of health-promoting qualities of leafy greens, and never once did I hear his nemesis, Bluto, ask him where he gets his protein.

Even if you don't have Bluto to contend with every day, I hope this chapter will give you the knowledge and confidence to follow Popeye's example by making leafy greens a staple in your daily diet. Just lay off the Olive Oyl!

Green Protein

All leafy greens provide a healthy source of the essential amino acids (protein) required by the body. Eating sufficient calories through a variety of whole plant foods - especially leafy greens - will provide all the protein a person needs to build a strong, healthy body.

One of the many benefits of obtaining amino acids from whole plant foods, rather than animal flesh, is they are consumed in an anti-inflammatory matrix of fiber, water, vitamins, minerals, and antioxidants. Whereas, the protein from cooked flesh is largely denatured in the cooking process and is consumed in a pro-inflammatory agglomeration of saturated fat, heterocyclic amines (HCAs), and bacterial endotoxins.

Biomagnification of environmental pollutants (pesticides, heavy metals, industrial chemicals, etc.) is another reason to choose plants over animal flesh when sourcing your protein. Cows, for example, regularly consume various toxins through their unnatural diet of GMO feed crops, bone meal, animal blood, and other discarded parts of pigs, fish, chickens, horses, cats, and dogs that are deemed unfit for human consumption.

The livestock industry discovered that a combination of grains and animal protein would fatten cattle up faster and get them to market sooner. Over the span of the cow's life, the concentration of these toxins continues to magnify in its flesh. Once that cow ends up on your plate, it could contain astronomical levels of toxicity!

Plants, on the other hand, are at the bottom of the food chain and do not biomagnify toxins in their flesh. To put it simply, there is no cleaner source of protein for the human body than plants!

Some of the higher protein leafy greens include kale, spinach, and collard greens. Consider incorporating these, and other leafy greens into your salads, smoothies, and juices to increase your protein intake without the downsides of animal products.

Calcium

Contrary to what many people think, cows do not make calcium. Calcium is a mineral in the soil that ends up in the grass that cows graze on all day. So, instead of drinking the breast milk of a cow, why not get our calcium from the same place the cows do - greens!

Leafy greens can be a great source of calcium, which is vital for strong bones and teeth, as well as supporting muscle function and the nervous system.

Some leafy greens like spinach, beet greens, and chard contain higher levels of oxalates, which bind to calcium and prevent it from being absorbed into the body. So even though these are nutritious and healthy leafy greens with other health benefits, we only absorb about 5% of their calcium.

To get the most calcium out of your greens, it may be best to focus more on low-oxalate leafy greens, such as kale, lettuces, collard greens, mustard greens, turnip greens, and bok choy.

Iron

Leafy greens are also a good source of iron, which is an essential nutrient for healthy red blood cells and energy production. Plant foods contain non-heme iron, which is a form of iron that the body is efficient at regulating its absorption based on the body's current iron needs.

Iron from animal products is referred to as heme iron and is absorbed into the body in a much less controlled fashion. Consuming heme iron puts a person at a higher risk of iron overload, resulting in increased oxidative damage and chronic disease over time. This is why non-heme iron is the ideal form of iron to consume for long-term health and longevity.

Leafy greens that are especially rich in iron, include dandelion greens, kale, butter lettuce, parsley, and spinach. Consuming your greens with Vitamin C-rich foods has been shown to optimize the absorption of non-heme iron. This can be done by adding greens to a fruit smoothie or simply using lemon in your salad dressing.

Other ways to optimize iron absorption are by consuming your leafy greens with allium vegetables (garlic, onions, etc.), as well as beta-carotene-rich foods (carrots, tomatoes, etc.).

Magnesium

If it's green, think magnesium! Magnesium is the central element in chlorophyll, the green pigment in plants. In the human body, magnesium is an essential mineral and electrolyte that plays a key role in many of the body's functions.

Magnesium acts as a cofactor in hundreds of metabolic reactions in the body, including the regulation of heart rate, blood pressure, and muscle and nerve function. It is also critical for maintaining strong bones and supporting healthy immune function.

Eating more leafy greens is a great way to increase the magnesium content of your diet. The leafy greens highest in magnesium include spinach, kale, beet greens, and Swiss chard.

Vitamin C

Oranges are not the only source of vitamin C in a plant-based diet. You may be surprised to learn that leafy greens have a surprising amount of this vital antioxidant!

Vitamin C helps to protect cells from oxidative damage caused by free radicals. It is also essential for the production of collagen, which is needed for healthy skin, bones, and connective tissue.

Leafy greens such as kale, Swiss chard, and arugula can provide up to 100% of the daily recommended intake of vitamin C per 100 grams.

Folate (Vitamin B9)

Folate is an essential B vitamin required for cellular formation, division, and function, as well as the synthesis of amino acids and DNA.

Deficiencies in folate can cause elevated homocysteine levels in the blood, which can lead to inflammation and plaque formation in the arteries - increasing the risk of heart attack and stroke.

It's important to know that folate is not the same thing as folic acid. Folic acid is the synthetic version of folate used in supplements and has been linked to cancer! Getting folate from natural sources, like leafy greens, is the safest and most effective way to fulfill your folate needs.

Men and women ages 19 years and older are recommended to aim for 400 mcg per day. Pregnant and lactating women are advised to increase their intake to 600 mcg per day. Leafy greens are one of the richest sources of folate and other B vitamins. 100 grams of raw spinach provides roughly 194 mcg of folate.

Other leafy greens high in folate include mustard greens, turnip greens, collard greens, and romaine lettuce. Like other B vitamins, folate is degraded by heat processing and storage time - so eat your greens as fresh and raw as possible in order to maximize your folate intake.

Vitamin K

Vitamin K is a group of fat-soluble vitamins that are needed for proper blood clotting and bone mineralization. K1 (phylloquinone) and K2 (menaquinone) are the two main forms of this vitamin.

K1 is the predominant form that we obtain from our diet and is mainly found in green vegetables. In the liver, K1 is used to activate clotting factors in the blood.

K2 is synthesized by our gut bacteria, and can also be found in fermented foods, such as nato, due to the bacterial nature of these foods. K2 plays an important role in directing dietary calcium into our bones, rather than into the artery walls or other soft tissue.

The recommended daily intake for K1 in adults is 120 mcg, which can be achieved by eating just 1 1/4 cups of kale or 1 cup of spinach. There is no established requirement to consume K2 when our K1 requirements have been met. So, as long as we eat enough K1 from plants, our gut bacteria should take care of any K2 needs that we may have. This is yet another reason to maintain a healthy gut microbiome.

Green leafy vegetables such as kale, Brussels sprouts, parsley, collard greens, broccoli, spinach, cabbage, and lettuce are all great sources of vitamin K1.

Omega-3s

When discussing essential fats, most of the attention is given to walnuts, flax seeds, chia seeds, and hemp seeds for their higher concentrations of the omega-3 fatty acid, alpha-linolenic acid (ALA). While those are all great sources of ALA, leafy greens can also be a significant source of this nutrient as well.

The Food and Nutrition Board of the Institute of Medicine (IOM) recommends women get 1.1g of ALA and 1.6g for men. This is certainly achievable with a diet based on whole fruits, vegetables, leafy greens, and a small number of seeds.

Two medium heads of romaine lettuce (roughly 125 calories worth) will provide about 1g of ALA. Outside of that, if you were to eat about 1,000 calories of fresh fruits and vegetables, you would also get about 1g of ALA. So, a fruit and vegetable-based diet, with an emphasis on leafy greens, should comfortably satisfy the recommended intake for ALA.

For the best overall omega-3 levels, it is wise to avoid processed foods, nut butter, and high-fat diets, due to their inhibition of the body's conversion rates of turning ALA into long-chain omega-3 fats, EPA and DHA.

Nitrates

Nitrates are naturally occurring compounds found in plants grown in nitrogen-rich soil. These compounds have been shown to have a variety of cardiovascular health benefits.

Nitrates are reduced into nitrites via the saliva in the mouth and then reduced further in the stomach and blood vessels into nitric oxide. Nitric oxide helps to relax and dilate blood vessels, leading to improved blood flow and lower blood pressure. Nitrates have also gained attention for improving athletic performance by drinking nitrate-rich beet juice.

Leafy greens such as spinach, arugula, and lettuce are among the foods highest in nitrates, making them an excellent dietary source of these beneficial compounds.

It is important to note that the nitrate content of leafy greens can vary depending on growing conditions and cooking methods, so eating a variety of leafy greens and eating them raw or lightly cooked can help to optimize nitrate intake.

Prebiotic Fibers

The human gut is only as strong as the microbes that reside within it. The composition and diversity of the microbe population within the gut are dependent on the type of material that moves through the digestive tract.

Prebiotic fibers from fruits and vegetables feed probiotic bacteria, which then produce powerful postbiotic compounds essential for the health of the gut and body.

Prebiotic fibers are a type of non-digestible fiber that is fermented by beneficial bacteria in the gut. This fermentation process produces powerful compounds called short-chain fatty acids (SCFA), which provide nourishment for the cells that line the colon and help to maintain a healthy gut barrier. SCFAs provide an important source of fuel for beneficial gut bacteria while suppressing the growth of pathogenic species.

By consuming leafy greens and other sources of prebiotic fibers, you can support the growth of beneficial bacteria in the gut, reduce inflammation, improve insulin sensitivity, support the immune system, and improve overall health throughout the body.

Chlorophyll

In today's high-stress and heavily polluted environments, leafy greens play an important role in alkalizing the body and supporting detoxification. One way they do this is through the action of chlorophyll, a pigment that gives plants their green color. Chlorophyll has powerful antioxidant properties, which help to protect cells from damage caused by reactive oxygen species (ROS) or free radicals.

When we consume leafy greens, chlorophyll decreases the number of ROS that are naturally produced by our cell's mitochondria as they go about their daily functions. High levels of ROS lead to oxidative stress and damage to the cells, leading to inflammation and accelerated aging throughout the body.

Reactive oxygen species, such as superoxide, are like clouds of toxic gasses that continuously flow from the smokestacks of power plants, polluting the surrounding environment.

A chlorophyll-rich diet helps to transform the mitochondria into high-efficiency, energy-producing factories. In other words, the cells can produce more energy at a lower cost, with less waste. This allows the body to direct more of its vital resources to support other biological tasks.

Leafy greens such as kale, spinach, and parsley are among the foods highest in chlorophyll.

Detoxification Support

Once in the digestive tract, fiber and chlorophyll are highly effective at binding to toxins and preventing them from being absorbed into the body. These toxins include carcinogens, such as polycyclic aromatic hydrocarbons (PAHs), heterocyclic amines, and aflatoxin, as well as heavy metals, bile acids, cholesterol, and hormones, like estrogen.

Once bound to fiber or chlorophyll, the toxins are effectively eliminated from the body, one bowel movement at a time. The timely removal of these compounds helps to reduce inflammation, support a healthy gut microbiome, and maintain the integrity of the intestinal wall.

Leafy greens also provide benefits to the liver, which plays a central role in the body's detoxification process. Cruciferous leafy greens (kale, cabbage, arugula, etc.) contain compounds known as glucosinolates that when chewed, mix with the enzyme myrosinase, to form isothiocyanate compounds, such as sulforaphane.

Sulforaphane is known to induce phase II detoxification enzymes from the liver that convert toxic substances (drugs, hormones, pollutants, etc.) into water-soluble compounds that can be more safely removed from the body via the urine.

The presence of sulforaphane also increases the liver's production of the powerful antioxidant, glutathione – which has numerous protective and detoxification-enhancing properties.

Between chlorophyll, fiber, hydration, isothiocyanates, vitamin C, and the powerful alkalizing effects of leafy greens - it's no wonder why these superfoods are so effective at supporting the body's cleansing efforts from head to toe.

Cognitive Function

The brain is a highly vascular organ, reported to receive 15-20% of the body's blood supply at any given time. If the brain does not receive adequate oxygen and nutrition from a steady flow of blood, brain cells will die, and cognitive function will decline.

As we learned earlier, leafy greens are one of the best foods for the health of the vascular system. Loaded with beneficial nutrients such as chlorophyll, folate, magnesium, antioxidants, and nitrates - leafy greens are like the Swiss army knife of cognitive protection.

Two of the most prominent benefits leafy greens impart on the brain and body are the increased production of nitric oxide and powerful antioxidant effects.

Nitric oxide not only helps blood to flow smoothly through blood vessels but also acts as a neurotransmitter in the brain and central nervous system. So, while it keeps blood and nutrients flowing through the brain, it is simultaneously facilitating neurological communication throughout the body.

While the brain only represents about two percent of our body mass, it consumes an estimated twenty percent of our total energy supply. With all that activity, there are a lot of reactive oxygen species (free radicals) produced, which can damage surrounding tissues if it is not accounted for.

This is where the antioxidant abilities of leafy greens shine. Lutein, zeaxanthin, beta-carotene, vitamin C, and others help the body respond to reactive oxygen species and neutralize their harmful effects. They also increase the body's production of a neurotransmitter called brain-derived neurotrophic factor (BDNF), which plays an essential role in the health and longevity of neurons, as well as learning and memory.

To put it simply, leafy greens should be top of mind for anyone concerned with healthy cognition.

Weight Optimization

Leafy greens have two unique qualities that make them especially helpful for optimizing body weight. First, besides being packed with fiber, water, vitamins, and minerals - they also contain what are known as thylakoids.

Thylakoids are tiny membrane-bound compartments in the leaves of plants that help absorb sunlight in order for photosynthesis to occur.

These little membranes bind to our body's fat-digesting enzyme, lipase, and cause a delay in the absorption of fats. Due to the effects of thylakoids, fats are broken down and absorbed in the distal end of the small intestine, triggering a phenomenon called the "ileal brake." This mechanism causes satiety (fullness) hormones to increase and hunger hormones to decrease - allowing us to feel full on significantly fewer calories.

Not only can thylakoids reduce hunger, but they have also been shown to reduce cravings and blunt the pleasure response when eating processed foods.

Thylakoid membranes contain the green pigment, chlorophyll - so the greener the leaves, the more thylakoids in your meal!

The second weight-optimizing quality leafy greens offer is having the lowest caloric density of any other whole food. Containing only about 100 calories per pound, leafy greens can fill you up with their bulky fiber and water content, while contributing very few calories to your overall diet.

Calorie Density

(500 calories in the stomach)

OIL **CHEESE** **MEAT** **POTATOES, BEANS, RICE** **FRUITS, VEGGIES**

Caloric density refers to the number of calories in a given amount of food. It is calculated by dividing the number of calories in a food by its weight.

Below you will see that foods with a caloric density of 600 calories per pound or less are displayed in green. These foods are high in fiber, water, and micro-nutrients, which make them ideal foods for weight management.

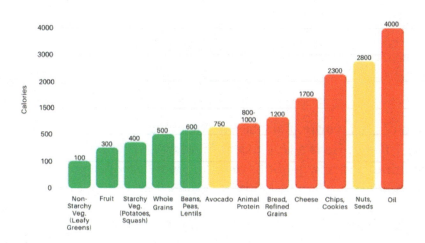

Foods displayed in yellow are still healthy, whole plant foods, however, they are higher in fat and caloric density and should be eaten in smaller amounts.

Low-calorie-dense foods, like leafy greens, promote feelings of fullness, reduce overall calorie intake, and allow you to eat more food and weigh less!

Understanding the principles of caloric density can be a useful tool for making informed dietary choices that will help you achieve your optimal body weight.

2

Greens In Abundance

One of my favorite plant-based doctors is Dr. Caldwell Esselstyn Jr. He is a true example, at age 89, of the powerful health-enhancing qualities of eating leafy green vegetables in abundance.

Dr. Esselstyn is known for his love of leafy greens and admits that he "adores when his patients have an evening snack of kale." He prescribes his patients with heart disease consume at least six fist-sized portions of leafy greens daily.

Dr. Esselstyn says nothing beats the antioxidant value of green leafy vegetables. His goal is for his patients to bathe the insides of their inflamed blood vessels with a cascade of powerful antioxidants, chiefly nitric oxide.

Through his plant-based protocol and award-winning work in the field of cardiology, Dr. Esselstyn has become one of the most well-respected voices in the whole food, plant-based movement, and in medicine.

An extensive 2016 meta-analysis titled, *The effect of green leafy and cruciferous vegetable intake on the incidence of cardiovascular disease* reviewed the previous twenty-five years of relevant global research and found that:

> *"A high daily intake of green leafy vegetables significantly reduced the incidence of several types of cardiovascular disease."*

There are close to 1,000 different species of plants with edible leaves that we know of. Each variety offers a unique nutritional profile that we can benefit from.

That said, unless you are foraging or growing your own, you will be limited to whatever is at the grocery store. Though, even if you obtain all of your greens from the grocery store, there is still an abundance of variety to choose from.

To give you an idea of what leafy greens you can find in most grocery stores, Dr. Esselstyn crafted this list and often tunefully recites it as his signature jingle:

Bok choy, Swiss chard, kale, collards, collard greens, beet greens, mustard greens, turnip greens, napa cabbage, Brussel sprouts, broccoli, cauliflower, cilantro, parsley, spinach, arugula, and asparagus - and his top five favorites are kale, swiss chard, spinach, arugula, beet greens (and beets.)

In addition to Dr. Essylstein's list above, you will likely find many of the following greens at your local markets:

Aloe	Artichoke	Basil
Butter lettuce	Celery	Coriander

Dill	Endive	Escarole
Fennel	Green leaf lettuce	Green cabbage
Iceberg lettuce	Kohlrabi greens	Purple cabbage
Radicchio	Radish greens	Red leaf lettuce
Romaine lettuce	Spring greens	Spring onion

Since many leafy green vegetables are heavily sprayed with a variety of toxic pesticides, I recommend choosing organic greens as much as possible. If you only have the option to buy non-organic greens, just do the best you can.

Soaking vegetables in purified water and baking soda (1 tsp for every 2 cups of water) for 15-20 minutes can help to remove some of the pesticide residues. It is probably wise to do this with organic produce as well.

I also suggest buying as many of your leafy greens as loose heads or bunches rather than boxed or bagged greens. Loose bunches are generally fresher than boxed greens, and it creates less plastic waste in the world.

If your local grocery store doesn't carry a lot of leafy greens, speak with the produce manager and ask if they can add to their inventory, or see if they can special order specific greens for you. If they are unable to do so, search out the nearest food coop, health food store, Asian market, or farmer's market.

Food coops and farmer's markets will be your best bet for finding the best quality organic leafy greens in your area. Asian markets often have a wider variety of lesser-known greens than your standard grocery store or food coop.

Wild Edibles

In addition to what you can find in grocery stores, there is likely an abundance of wild edible leafy greens growing in your local environment. Foraging for wild greens can be a fun and exciting way to add an even wider variety of greens to your diet.

Below are just a few of the nutritious wild edible plants that you may have growing right beneath your feet!

Amaranth	Black mustard	Black nightshade
Chickweed	Chicory	Charlock
Chives	Dandelion	Fiddlehead greens
Lambs quarters	Mallow	Mache
Mint	Miner's lettuce	Plantain
Pokeweed	Sow thistle	Stinging nettle
Water spinach	Watercress	Wild sorrel

The golden rule of foraging is to only eat something if you are 100% certain of what it is. Wild foraging should only be done with experienced guidance, as some wild plants can be toxic. Look for guided wild foraging hikes in your area or you can find numerous books written by experts on this topic. Starting out with some of the easiest-to-identify species, such as dandelion, or plantain can be a great way to get your feet wet with foraging.

There are numerous benefits to including wild edible plants in your diet. They are often much higher in vitamins, minerals, and overall nutrition than even certified organic produce due to deeper root systems, growing in richer soils, and surviving in harsh environmental conditions. Just like people, plants become stronger and more resilient when they overcome challenging situations. If we are what we eat - shouldn't we all strive to be more resilient like "weeds?"

Wild edibles will add new, delicious flavors and textures to your meals that you have never experienced before. No matter your culinary skill level, you can have fun creating new recipes with these nutrient-packed gifts from nature. Blend them into a smoothie, toss them in a salad, or add them to savory vegetable soups to get started.

Another great benefit to wild foraged plants is they are likely to be completely free of any kind of pesticides, as long as you're foraging in an unmaintained area. This is another reason why wild foraging can be even more health-promoting than even eating standard organic produce from a store.

While certified organic produce is not allowed to be sprayed with most synthetic pesticides, like glyphosate, they are still allowed to be sprayed with other approved pesticides that are deemed to be safer.

What's obvious is government regulatory agencies cannot be trusted to determine or recommend what is truly safe for public health, so it is best to be proactive and buy from local farmers you trust, forage your own wild edibles, and grow your own food as much as possible.

Be very aware of your surroundings when foraging. Always take into account if there are nearby roads, heavily used paths where people bring their animals, and other potential sources of contamination. If you are planning to forage on someone else's property or at a public park, always do your homework and call ahead to find out if they use any pesticides and where they spray them.

Maybe the most motivating factor of all is wild edibles are free! They cost you nothing, other than your time and the resources to get to wherever you are going to forage. With the effects of rising inflation on the cost of living, there are more reasons than ever to learn how to identify free food in nature and grow our own.

There is immense power in knowing how to find and grow your own food. We have become much too reliant on grocery stores to feed ourselves and it is time we relearn a basic but valuable skill that could one day save your life.

Indoor and Outdoor Gardening

You don't need a green thumb or a large garden to be successful at growing your own greens and other produce. A productive garden can come in all shapes and sizes. Whether you have a plot of land, a small balcony, a sunny window sill, or just a small space on your countertop, you can start growing a significant amount of greens and reap the benefits of this healthy and fulfilling practice.

If you are new to growing food, a great first step is to connect with experienced gardeners in your area through gardening classes, local nurseries, community gardens, and farmer's markets. Books and online groups can also help teach you the foundational knowledge needed to have a successful gardening experience.

Outdoor Gardens

When planting an outdoor garden, first, you will need to determine what crops you want to grow. It's also important to learn the basics of building healthy soil, watering methods, positioning your garden for the best sunlight, what plants grow best in your specific climate, and the best time of year to plant each species.

One of the many benefits of growing your food is that you are able to grow varieties that you can't find in grocery stores. This allows you to expand the abundance of greens and other fruits and vegetables in your diet even further.

It is best to start with plant varieties that are easy to grow in your area and produce a high yield. To make it even easier, you can buy starter plants from a local nursery or farmer's market where they have already grown the plant to a couple of inches tall, and you can transplant those directly into your garden. This will increase the chances of having a successful crop versus growing everything directly from seed.

Below are five of the easiest salad greens to grow for beginners:

1. Kale
2. Spinach
3. Arugula
4. Mustard greens
5. Lettuce

Potted Herbs

If you are not in a position to have an outdoor garden, you can still grow a variety of potted herbs on any sunny window sill or countertop. Fresh herbs can be grown indoors year-round, and they add incredible flavor and nutrition to any meal.

Just as with growing an outdoor garden, you'll first need to decide which crops you want to grow. Luckily, most indoor herbs all do well under the same basic growing conditions:

- Light, loose, airy, neutral to slightly acidic pH, moist, nutrient-rich, and sterile soil. Any store-bought mix designed for container gardening will work.
- Watering roughly once per week (or enough to keep to soil moist but not soggy). The soil should never completely dry out, but do not over-water!
- A four to six-inch diameter terra cotta or stainless steel pot with a depth of at least 6 inches (must have drainage holes) is a good choice for indoor herbs. Give each plant its own container for the easiest long-term maintenance.
- At least six hours of full-spectrum light daily is best.
- A steady temperature of around 70 degrees Fareheight should keep most herbs happy.
- Regular harvesting or trimming will keep the plant from going to seed (the end of its life cycle) and growing healthfully. Besides, with basil, do not harvest more than about 1/4 of the plant at one time to avoid shocking and potentially killing it.
- A water-soluble organic liquid kelp fertilizer can be used once a month to help keep your plants healthy.

These are just general tips that can help you get started with your indoor herb garden, so I recommend doing further research to gain a deeper understanding of how to achieve the best results.

Five of the best herbs to start growing indoors include:

1. Basil
2. Cilantro

3. Chives
4. Arugula
5. Dill

Microgreens

If you want to take your indoor gardening a step further, microgreens are where it's at. Microgreens are just as the name implies - tiny greens. They are the seedlings of various vegetables and herbs that are harvested anywhere from one to four weeks of age. These young plants can be easy to grow, and they come packed with super nutrition, freshness, and outstanding flavor.

Microgreens contain significantly higher concentrations of many nutrients compared to their adult counterparts, making them an excellent addition to any meal. High-end chefs have been using microgreens for decades to add a fresh look and elegance to the meals they create in their restaurants. Nothing enhances the quality of a dish like the vibrancy of freshly grown microgreens.

Many health food stores now sell pre-harvested microgreens, but they are often quite expensive and don't have a long shelf-life. This makes growing your own a great option and does not require much space or maintenance. With a relatively small upfront investment in seeds, a growing medium, and containers, you could be harvesting fresh microgreens from your kitchen and adding life to your meals in just a few weeks.

Most people grow their microgreens in a standard 10x20-inch tray, but you can use whatever size of tray or container fits your needs.

In terms of depth, microgreens grow best in a shallow container (about 1 to 2 inches deep), and you will only need a thin layer of soil or other soilless media. Some growers choose to purchase trays specifically designed for microgreens, and some get creative and use whatever flat containers they have lying around that can hold soil.

If you are using soil, sterilized varieties are recommended for indoor growing to prevent mold, fungal spores, or any other harmful organisms you could encounter using compost or soil from an outdoor garden.

Other popular growing medium options include hemp fiber mats, coconut coir, biostrate, and hydroponic methods, to name a few. Each of these methods has pros and cons, so you will need to determine which one you think will work best for your goals and living conditions.

When it's time to start planting:

- Add your chosen growing medium (soil, etc.) evenly into the container, leaving about a half-inch from the soil to the top of the container - don't fill it all the way to the top. Some growers prefer to add a little water to the bottom of the tray before adding in the soil to help prevent mold occurrence.
- Next, spread a fairly dense single layer of seeds evenly over the growing medium.
- Then, go ahead and carefully mist the seeds and soil (if that's what you're using) with water enough to moisten everything fully but not enough to create standing water.
- Then, place a cover over the seeds and place them in a safe place for the next two or three days to germinate.

Once the germination process has finished, you will need to keep the seeds covered from light for the next two or three days while the seeds root themselves into the growing medium. Some seeds do better with a small amount of weight placed on the cover to put pressure on the seeds as they start to grow upwards. This mimics the environment under the soil that the seeds would normally be in if they were growing in nature.

Next, you can remove the cover and expose the microgreens to light, which will allow them to start greening up through the process of photosynthesis. Microgreens should get at least six to eight hours of natural sunlight or twelve to eighteen hours of artificial light each day. If there is insufficient exposure, the microgreens will not turn out as vibrant and flavorful as they could have under proper lighting. Many microgreens will do great just sitting next to a sunny window, but if needed, supplemental lighting can be provided using fluorescent or LED lights.

Continue misting with water (or look into bottom watering) twice a day or as needed to keep the growing medium moist, and prevent the roots from drying out. Within one to four weeks (depending on the species) your healthy and delicious crop will be ready to harvest.

Once again, this is by no means an extensive growing guide, so I recommend doing more research on the best growing practices for whatever variety of microgreens you choose to grow.

Some of the most popular microgreens to grow for beginners include:

1. Radish
2. Sunflower

3. Broccoli
4. Pea shoots
5. Mustard greens

Sprouts

The younger brother of microgreens and an even easier method of growing food is sprouts! Sprouting is the ultimate beginner crop for anyone looking to add more greens and abundance to their diet.

Sprouts are similar to microgreens, but they are harvested just a few days after germination. Most sprouts require no soil or growing medium and can be eaten as soon as you see the tail emerge from the seed. It is generally recommended to harvest once the tail is about one to two inches long and the hulls have been shed from the seeds.

Just like microgreens, sprouts are an incredibly nutrient-dense addition to any diet. Broccoli sprouts, for example, have been shown to contain 50-100 times the levels of certain nutrients than mature broccoli. In general, sprouts are highly concentrated sources of many vitamins, antioxidants, amino acids, and enzymes. Even if you are already eating a nutritionally sufficient diet with plenty of raw fruits and vegetables, sprouts add an element of life to the diet that you don't get anywhere else.

If you are worried that you don't have the skills, time, or money to invest in growing food, sprouts are by far the easiest, fastest, and most inexpensive means of improving your diet.

Growing sprouts is not just about eating more vegetables; it is an act of personal sovereignty and self-reliance. Anyone, regardless of their gardening knowledge, can grow an abundance of their own food in just a few days with a supply of seeds, clean water, and a container.

While there are a variety of methods for growing sprouts, including trays, hemp bags, clay pots, mason jars, and more - my favorite and preferred method (especially for beginners) is in a quart-sized mason jar with a straining lid (or cheesecloth).

My top sprouting seeds for beginners:

1. Green pea
2. Mung bean
3. Alfalfa
4. Green lentil
5. Broccoli

Here is a simple example of how to get started:

1. Select the type of seeds you would like to sprout. I recommend picking one from the list above.
2. Add your seeds of choice to a 1-quart mason jar. For larger seeds (green pea, mung bean, lentils), use 1/3 cup of seeds per batch. For smaller seeds, use 1/4 cup of seeds per batch.
3. Put a straining lid on the mason jar. These can be purchased online.
4. Fill the mason with enough purified water to cover the seeds in excess of about 2 inches. The seeds will significantly expand in size as they absorb the water. It is critical that they do not rise above the water level or they will not sprout properly.

5. Let the seeds soak for about 8 hours (overnight is the most convenient). There are sprouting seed soaking charts online, but I have always just used a general 8-hour standard for all of my seeds.
6. After 8 hours, drain the soak water and rinse the seeds with fresh water.
7. Now turn the jar mouth-end down and set it at about a 45-degree angle to allow the water to drain out and air to circulate throughout the jar.
8. You will need to rinse the seeds twice a day for the next 3 to 5 days - once in the morning and once before bed.
9. Throughout the process, keep the jar out of direct sunlight and in a place with good airflow.
10. The sprouts should never smell fermented, look slimy, or have mold growing on them. If they do, discard the batch and start over in a clean jar. This is less likely to happen if you follow these steps.
11. You can start eating the sprouts as soon as they have tails, but it is best to wait until the tails are at least an inch long for most sprouts.
12. On the last day before harvest, you can place the sprouts next to a sunny window to allow them to "green up" - especially for leafy sprouts like alfalfa or broccoli.

In addition to supporting your local organic farmers, growing and foraging your own greens empowers you to increase the abundance and diversity of your diet. Instead of the flat-head spinach that is ubiquitous in all grocery stores, you can grow longevity spinach or any of the dozens of other varieties of spinach that Nature offers.

You'll likely never see lamb's quarters at the store, but once you learn to identify it, there is a good chance that you have access to it for free in your environment, along with countless other edible wild plants.

Whether you are foraging, gardening, or sprouting, you are enhancing your connection with Nature and God, and you will reap the physical, emotional, and spiritual benefits that come with it.

If your goal is to be as healthy as possible in body, mind, and spirit, then make it a goal to eat a minimum of one pound of leafy green vegetables every day with as much variety and living food as you can.

Domestic Diversity Vs Natural Abundance

The level of dietary diversity optimal for human health is an ongoing topic of debate. Some believe that it's best to eat one food at a time and that a relatively narrow range of foods is all we need, while others point to research suggesting a more diverse diet is associated with health and longevity. The truth may be somewhere in the middle.

In this section, I will share some general thoughts and ideas for you to consider when determining how diverse you want your diet to be.

It is estimated that there are more than 400,000 species of plants on Earth, with more than half of them being edible for humans - yet worldwide, we cultivate and consume only about 200 of these edible species. What's more, most Americans regularly eat fewer than 30 species and more than half of the calories we obtain from plants come from just four species: corn, wheat, rice, and potato.

Compare that to the more than 113 different plant species that our primate cousins are eating, and it shows just how limited our diets have become.

There is no question that industrialized agriculture has both benefits and drawbacks. One of the drawbacks is that it can reduce the depth of diversity in what the average person eats. For example, there are at least 45 different varieties of carrots, however, you will likely find only one variety in most stores.

You also end up with many products made from the same cheap ingredients, such as corn, and wheat. So, even though someone is buying a variety of products, they are eating the same ingredients, just with different artificial flavors.

The foods being grown for grocery store shelves are not generally chosen for their nutritional content or health benefits - they are mainly selected for their economic value and productivity.

So, unless you are growing heirloom or other uncommon varieties at home, you will be limited to the few varieties of fruits and vegetables that are most profitable to the industry.

On the other hand, transportation and international commerce advancements *have* made it possible to enjoy far more diversity than ever before. We now have an assortment of tropical and subtropical fruits available to us year-round, even during the frigid winters in Minnesota.

Out of curiosity, I went to my local grocery store to see how many different species of fresh plants I could find. I counted over 110 different varieties between fruits, vegetables, nuts, and seeds. Unfortunately, what I saw in people's grocery carts made it clear that very few of these fruits and vegetables are being consumed.

The Sad American Diet

According to the United States Department of Agriculture, in 2019, the vast majority of people's vegetable consumption came from potatoes and tomatoes in the form of french fries and pizza sauce. Other notable vegetables consumed in much smaller quantities included onions, carrots, corn, and head lettuce.

The bulk of Americans' fruit consumption came from apples and oranges - mostly as bottled juices. Bananas, grapes, and watermelon were also among the most commonly eaten fruits.

The sad reality is that much of people's fruit and vegetable intake comes in a processed form, which is often ushered into their mouths via some form of genetically modified breading or high-fructose corn syrup-based sauce.

It is imperative that people and their families become educated about the vital importance of consuming a variety of fresh, whole, and natural plant foods to support physical and mental well-being.

Even many people on a whole food plant-based diet lack variety in what they eat. Similar to those eating a standard American diet, plant-based eaters find a few foods they enjoy and only buy those foods week after week. It is great to have structure and consistency in the way we eat but also including variation and rotating through a wider range of whole plant foods is likely a good idea.

Humans are biologically a tropical species, which would suggest that we are designed to eat a tropical diet. Tropical rainforests are known for their extreme depth of biodiversity in both plant and animal life. They are home to half of all the living animal and plant species on the planet.

With many thousands of wild edible plants growing in these forests, wouldn't we naturally be eating a highly diverse diet of tropical fruits, leafy greens, and other plant matter - similar to wild primates?

While grocery stores may not have the same depth and diversity as rainforests, there are still well over 100 different varieties of plants that we can enjoy if we choose to take advantage of what is available. So, by incorporating more of what is offered at the grocery store, we can potentially come close to matching the same amount of variety that other primates are consuming.

Fresh Is Best

I do not believe all the power lies in variety alone. It is important to consider that many relatively long-lived, healthy people have sustained themselves a relatively narrow diet. However, most often these people were also living active lifestyles filled with purpose and eating plenty of fresh foods. The freshness of our food seems to be another key factor in producing long-term health.

In the context of food, I define "fresh" as food that was harvested within the last week. When food is truly fresh, it contains the highest levels of vital energy that it obtains from its connection with the Earth - like a cell phone battery with a full charge. Most foods we buy at the grocery store are harvested weeks or months earlier and have considerably less vitality. Just because a food is raw, does not mean that it is fresh.

The importance of including foraged and homegrown plants in the diet is not just about adding variety but even more vital, it is about increasing the freshness of the food we eat.

Variety and freshness work synergistically to nourish and empower the body and mind to function at their optimal levels - so it is essential that we do not neglect either of these factors in our diet.

Plants Educate the Body

The final consideration regarding dietary diversity pertains to a fundamental function of food. In addition to providing the raw materials required to run the body, food is a source of information.

Plants contain various components that influence the body's genetic expression, immune function, microbiome status, and much more. A wider variety of plants in the diet gives the body a much deeper understanding of how to best adapt and thrive in its environment - especially when they are grown locally.

We can maximize the body's intelligence by bringing in more fresh, wild, and homegrown plant foods into our diets using the various options discussed in this book. By doing this, we not only fuel and educate our bodies with the best available information, but we establish a relationship with the incredible abundance of Nature.

Humans are currently surviving on only about 0.0001% of the edible plants in existence - talk about an abundant world!

However diverse you choose to make your diet, do your best to emphasize the *freshness* of the foods you eat.

3

Clean Greens

We often hear the phrase, "clean eating" used by various diet groups to describe their version of healthy eating. I cannot tell you how many times I have seen this phrase used to describe some of the dirtiest foods that people eat. When I say dirty food, I don't mean food that has dirt on it. Dirty food is toxic food; food that is saturated with invisible chemicals that damage the body, as well as the environment. Even the healthiest foods can be made into dirty foods, depending on how they are produced.

Conventionally grown leafy greens are among the dirtiest crops someone can eat. According to the Environmental Working Group's 2022 report, a single sample of kale, collard, and mustard greens had up to 21 different pesticides. Spinach samples averaged 1.8 times as much pesticide residue by weight as any other crop tested.

Depending on the sample being tested, leafy greens can have anywhere from 2 to more than 100 detectible pesticides. The pesticide most frequently detected on collards, mustard greens, and kale is DCPA (sold as Dacthal) – which is classified by the EPA as a possible human carcinogen and was banned by the EU in 2009. Neurotoxic neonicotinoids and pyrethroids are also common pesticides found on leafy greens.

What's The Problem With Pesticides?

A more accurate name for these chemicals is biocides - meaning **to destroy life**. Pesticide is an umbrella term for the various products intended to prevent, repel, or kill "pest organisms." Just a few of the more well-known pesticides include insecticides (insects), herbicides (weeds), fungicides (fungi), bactericides (bacteria), avicides (birds), and rodenticides (rodents). As you can see, in the eyes of big industry, everything and everyone is a potential pest to be eliminated.

One of the many problems with pesticides is that they are not target specific. Billions of pounds of these chemicals are sprayed every year, saturating our soils and ending up in the water supply.

In the soil, these chemicals are detrimental to the highly susceptible earthworm populations, causing immobility, death, and reproductive harm. Not only does this cause catastrophic damage to soil biodiversity, but these chemicals bioaccumulate within the worms, which then become contaminated food for many fish, reptiles, amphibians, birds, and small mammals.

Pollinator species such as bees and butterflies are killed in massive numbers by various insecticides, like neonicotinoids. When it rains, pesticides run off into our waterways, killing fish and other aquatic life. Many of these sprays can also volatilize and drift several hundred miles in the wind affecting anyone and anything in their path.

The numerous health effects on humans and wildlife are well-known and documented. A 2013 scientific review article published in the Journal of Toxicology and Applied Pharmacology, stated:

> "There is a huge body of evidence on the relation between exposure to pesticides and elevated rates of chronic diseases such as different types of cancers, diabetes, neurodegenerative disorders like Parkinson, Alzheimer, and amyotrophic lateral sclerosis (ALS), birth defects, and reproductive disorders.
>
> There is also circumstantial evidence of the association of exposure to pesticides with some other chronic diseases like respiratory problems, particularly asthma and chronic obstructive pulmonary disease (COPD), cardiovascular diseases, chronic nephropathies, autoimmune diseases like systemic lupus erythematous and rheumatoid arthritis, chronic fatigue syndrome, and aging.
>
> The common feature of chronic disorders is a disturbance in cellular homeostasis, which can be induced via pesticides' primary action like perturbation of ion channels, enzymes, receptors, etc., or can as well be mediated via pathways other than the main mechanism."

By now you have probably heard of the popular herbicide glyphosate, which is known for its role as the active ingredient in the weed killer, Roundup. Not only has glyphosate been shown to **cause cancer**, but research is finding it has alarming consequences on the gut microbiome.

Glyphosate has been shown to disrupt a biochemical pathway called the shikimate pathway, which is used by plants and gut bacteria to produce important aromatic amino acids (tyrosine, phenylalanine, and tryptophan.) Without these essential amino acids, plants cannot survive and our gut bacteria cannot produce the amino acids we need to maintain health.

To make matters worse, glyphosate preferentially kills the beneficial probiotics in the gut and allows pathogenic species to proliferate. This contributes to inflammation and oxidative stress in the gut and throughout the body.

Another widely used herbicide, Atrazine, made headlines in the early 2000s when it was found to cause male frogs to develop female characteristics at levels 30 times lower than the allowable limit of 3 ppb in drinking water and 120 times lower than the proposed chronic exposure limit for aquatic life, 12 ppb.

The frogs exposed to atrazine had lower testosterone levels, produced less sperm, and changed their mating habits by choosing males over females. In humans, Atrazine has been shown to cause hormone dysregulation and damage to the nervous system, immune system, kidney, heart, and liver.

Besides the dangerous chemicals that we know are in these products, pesticides can contain "trade secret" chemical ingredients that aren't required to be disclosed or safety tested. Only the active ingredient (on its own) is required by the EPA to have safety testing done. That allows the adjuvants and "inactive" ingredients to be added without any data showing that it is safe. Not to mention, it is left up to the companies that profit from the approval and sale of these products to do the safety testing.

Non-Monotonic Dose Responses

If you have ever heard that pesticide residues are nothing to worry about because the amounts are too small to cause problems, let me tell you about non-monotonic dose responses.

When synthetic chemicals are encountered in very small doses, they can actually be even *more* toxic to the body than when exposed to larger amounts! This is called a non-monotonic dose response.

In very small concentrations, many of these chemicals act as hormone mimickers, or what are known as endocrine disruptors. This is a big problem because a disrupted endocrine (hormone) system can create a wide range of serious health problems and diseases.

Current safety testing methods are outdated and do not sufficiently assess the real-world toxicity of many chemicals.

Most safety testing focuses on a chemical's ability to cause cancer but fails to evaluate other important effects, such as endocrine disruption.

Standard testing guidelines falsely assume that high-dose testing can predict low-dose effects - which allows very toxic chemicals to pass safety tests and into the foods and products you and your family purchase.

The Cocktail Effect: 1 + 1 = 2,000

Another reason safety testing fails to determine the real-world toxicity of many chemicals is the fact that they do not analyze their synergistic effects when combined with other chemicals.

Companies are only required to conduct safety testing on the isolated "active ingredient" being used. This is a problem because the end-product that is sold to the consumer contains numerous other "inactive ingredients" that can (and do) alter how the "active ingredient" behaves and its potential health effects.

In the chemical world, 1 + 1 does not always equal 2. When multiple chemicals are combined, their degree of toxicity can increase by 1,000 times or more compared to their effects in isolation! This phenomenon is known as the "cocktail effect". **This is why it is dangerous to mix different household cleaners together, as they can react with each other to become even more lethal.**

So what happens when someone consumes multiple pesticide residues on top of the various pharmaceutical drugs and chemical-laden health and beauty products that people absorb into their bodies? Could this be contributing to the rise in chronic diseases and plummeting fertility rates?

To make things even more muddled, the "inactive ingredients" of a product are not required to be safety tested at all, nor are the mystery "trade secret" chemicals that are not even disclosed on the label. So when products, such as Roundup, are sprayed on crops, lawns, and parks, just remember that those chemicals have never been tested for safety as a combined formulation.

Toxicity Beyond Pesticides

Unfortunately, the potential for toxic contamination of our food, water, and environment does not *only* come from pesticides. There seems to be a contest throughout the various industries to see who can expose the public to the most toxic chemicals before they get a meaningless slap on the wrist from the captured "regulatory agencies."

It would take a separate book to cover all the sources that expose us to toxic chemicals. For the purpose of this book and the issues surrounding our food, I want to highlight a source of exposure that very few people are aware of: sewage sludge.

Sewage Sludge

Sewage sludge (also known as biosolids) is the noxious semi-solid gunk that is left over after separating out the liquid from raw sewage at municipal water treatment facilities. This raw sewage comes from homes, businesses, hospitals, funeral homes, slaughterhouses, industrial facilities, and roadside stormwater drains. Essentially everything that goes down a drain or toilet from any of these sources ends up in the sludge. This could include any of the following:

Pharmaceutical drugs	Steroids	Antibiotics
Hormones	Motor oil	Automobile exhaust chemicals
Disinfectants	Phthalates	PFAS (forever chemicals)
Synthetic fragrances	Industrial waste	Heavy metals
Pesticides	Dioxins	Polychlorinated biphenyls (PCBs)

Thousands of chemicals have been found in "biosolids," many of which are known to be toxic and persistent. These chemicals resist degradation once in the environment and can remain toxic to plants and animals for many decades or longer. Just like many pesticides, contamination from sewage sludge has been found in the roots, stems, leaves, fruits, and seeds that were fertilized with it.

The regulatory laws (Title 40 CFR Part 503) for biosolids were established in 1993, which are vastly outdated and unfit to protect the public and environment from harm. These rules only require 9 metals (arsenic, cadmium, copper, lead, mercury, molybdenum, nickel, selenium, and zinc) to be monitored in sludge used for land application - that's it! So if antibiotic-resistant bacteria have mutated in the sewage sludge that your conventional produce was grown in, don't expect the EPA to help you if you get sick.

Sewage sludge has been used as fertilizer on public parks, residential property, and conventional farmlands across the United States since at least the early 1990s. The crops fed to livestock are grown in it, it's commonly spread across active grazing pastures, and it's even mixed directly into livestock feed - those poor animals.

The positive news is that the USDA-certified organic standards prohibit the use of sewage sludge on organic farms. If you want to reduce your risk of exposure to toxic sewage sludge:

- Eat certified organic
- Eat a plant-exclusive diet
- Buy from local farmers you trust
- Grow your own food

If you grow your own food and are using store-bought compost or potting soil, you need to do your research on the soil you decide to buy. Many of the "natural," "eco-friendly," and even some "organic" bagged soils may contain biosolids, and it is not required to be listed on the package.

Some manufacturers disguise their use of biosolids on the ingredients list by using the term "compost." If you are unsure, it is best to contact the company or check the internet to see if the product in question uses biosolids.

Bagged soils that I trust are Dr. Earth Vegetarian Potting Soil and True Leaf Market's OMRI Potting Soil Mix. These two potting soils are organic and completely animal by-product free, which means they do not contain GMO-fed animal manures, feather meal, fish meal, shrimp meal, blood meal, bat guano, oyster shells, biosolids, or any other synthetic additives.

4

Green Myths

Even with all the evidence and research showing the wide range of health benefits we get from eating leafy green vegetables, there will always be contrarians!

It is hard to know the underlying motives behind some of the claims that are made, but keep in mind there are many diet camps and industries that profit from your fear and rejection of healthy food.

With that said, I know there are genuine questions and concerns that some people have regarding certain components of leafy greens.

I will do my best in this section to clear up the confusion and put many of the common myths about leafy greens to rest without going too far into the weeds - where most of these myths belong.

Alkaloids

Claim: Alkaloids are part of a plant's defense system and will harm your health and make you sick if you eat them.

What You Need To Know: Alkaloids are a class of naturally occurring organic compounds containing one or more nitrogen atoms. They are one reason why some plants have a bitter taste. These natural compounds are created by certain types of plants for what is believed to be a defense or deterrent against those who eat them.

There are thousands of known alkaloids, but a few that you are probably familiar with include:

- Morphine
- Nicotine
- Cocaine
- Caffeine
- Theobromine
- Solanine
- Capsaicin
- Oxalic acid

It is true that some plants contain alkaloids that can be fatal if consumed in large enough quantities. Then there are other alkaloids that, when consumed in whole-food form and in normal quantities, are believed to induce a hormetic (beneficial) response in the body.

Hormesis occurs when mild stress activates cellular signaling pathways, which lead to adaptations that create resistance to more severe stress in the future. Building muscle is an easy way to picture this process. When you frequently put your muscles through mild stress, over time, your body becomes stronger and more resilient.

Other classes of health-promoting phytonutrients, such as polyphenols, also elicit positive effects by causing low levels of hormetic stress in the body.

Alkaloids have long been valued for their therapeutic and medicinal effects, including:

Pain relief	Muscle relaxation	Stimulation
Anti-inflammatory	Antimicrobial	Anti-hypertensive
Anti-parasitic	Anti-tumor	Neuro-protective

One of the most sought-after plant medicines, ayahuasca, has psychoactive properties that are partly attributed to the alkaloid, **harmine**. If you are one of the 75% of Americans who wake up with a morning cup of coffee every day, you can thank the alkaloid, **caffeine**. And that slight "high" that some people get from chocolate, comes from the alkaloid, **theobromine**.

Many of the concerns over alkaloids pertain to the nightshade family of plants, which includes foods such as:

- Tomatoes
- Peppers
- Okra
- Eggplant
- White potatoes

While these are not leafy greens, they are staple salad ingredients for many people, so they are worth mentioning.

These foods (except tomatoes) contain an alkaloid called **solanine** which is believed to potentially be problematic for some individuals with active autoimmune conditions, such as rheumatoid arthritis. Tomatoes contain an alkaloid called **tomatine**, mainly in the plant's leaves, and stem, but also in small amounts in the fruit.

For the majority of people, tomatine and solanine-containing foods appear to be health-promoting additions to their diet. In fact, some research is finding that these compounds may have anti-cancer properties. This is not surprising, since these foods are rich in various vitamins, minerals, antioxidants, structured water, and fiber as well.

If you think you are sensitive to nightshades, consider removing them from your diet for two weeks, and then adding them back in one at a time and seeing if you notice any negative reactions.

What about the alkaloids in leafy greens, such as oxalic acid?

Oxalates

Claim: If you eat leafy greens, you will increase your risk of developing kidney stones.

What You Need To Know: Oxalic acid is an organic compound that is produced in the liver of mammals (including humans), and is found in almost all plants. It has a strong affinity for binding with minerals, including sodium, potassium, calcium, iron, and magnesium, which are then usually referred to as oxalate salts.

Dietary oxalic acid from plants is already bound to calcium and other minerals upon ingestion and generally does not get absorbed into the body. Research has shown that oxalates from plants do not significantly increase the oxalate load in the kidneys and that eating more fruits and vegetables leads to a decreased risk of developing kidney stones. In fact, it is animal products (meat, cheese, fish, eggs, milk, ice cream, etc.) and processed foods that are associated with a higher incidence of kidney stones.

A 2002 study in the New England Journal of Medicine titled, "Comparison of Two Diets for the Prevention of Recurrent Stones in Idiopathic Hypercalciuria" found that:

> "In men with recurrent calcium oxalate stones and hypercalciuria, restricted intake of animal protein and salt, combined with a normal calcium intake, provides greater protection than the traditional low-calcium diet."

Another study done on 83,922 postmenopausal women shows that they too should embrace a fruit and vegetable-based diet without worry about oxalates or increasing their risk of kidney stones.

This study was titled, "Dietary Intake of Fiber, Fruit, and Vegetables Decreases the Risk of Incident Kidney Stones in Women: A Women's Health Initiative Report" and concluded:

> "Greater dietary intake of fiber, fruits and vegetables were each associated with a reduced risk of incident kidney stones in postmenopausal women. The protective effects were independent of other known risk factors for kidney stones."

A 2004 study, titled "The Effect of Fruits and Vegetables on urinary stone risk factors" found that when fruits and vegetables are removed from the diet, the risk of kidney stones goes up:

> "Fruit and vegetable intake causes a dilution of lithogenic risk factors in the urine without affecting the concentration of potassium and citrate. Withdrawal of fruits and vegetables may expose even healthy subjects to the risk of developing renal calcium stones, whereas supplementing the diet with these food items might be helpful as a preventive measure in hypocitraturic stone formers.

Gut and kidney health play a critical role in the proper elimination of oxalates from the body. **Antibiotic use** can wipe out beneficial bacteria, such as Oxalobacter formigenes, Lactobacillus, and Bifidobacterium, which metabolize oxalates and help reduce oxalate levels in the body. In addition to avoiding antibiotic use as much as possible, a **high-fiber diet** is essential to maintain a balanced microbiome and overall gut health.

Animal protein, **saturated animal fat**, and **cholesterol** are known to impair kidney function and increase the risk of kidney stone formation. A 2014 study titled "Animal Protein and the Risk of Kidney Stones: A Comparative Metabolic Study of Animal Protein Sources" concluded that:

> "Consuming animal protein is associated with increased serum and urine uric acid in healthy individuals. The higher purine content of fish compared to beef or chicken is reflected in higher 24-hour urinary uric acid. However, as reflected in the saturation index, the stone forming propensity is marginally higher for beef compared to fish or chicken. Stone formers should be advised to limit the intake of all animal proteins, including fish."

In addition to consuming animal products and antibiotic use, the following factors could also increase a person's risk of developing kidney stones:

- Dehydration
- Antacid medications
- Calcium supplements
- Ascorbic acid (synthetic vitamin C) supplements
- High salt diets
- Processed food consumption
- Gastric bypass surgery
- Low fiber diets
- Laxative use
- Impaired gut lining
- Various pharmaceutical medications
- Obesity

Is it any wonder why more than half a million people go to the emergency room for kidney stones each year in the United States? The sooner people start eating more whole-plant foods, including plenty of leafy greens, fruits, and vegetables - the sooner we will see a reduction in the number of people suffering from kidney stones.

If you feel at risk for kidney stones, and you want to avoid high oxalate-containing leafy greens, the top three are:

1. Beet greens
2. Spinach
3. Chard

For anyone with a relatively healthy gut and healthy kidneys, there should be no concerns about the oxalates in leafy greens. Even for those with gut dysbiosis, leafy greens can help improve the health of the gut and overall protection from excessive oxalate absorption.

Goitrogens

Claim: Goitrogens in raw cruciferous vegetables will harm your thyroid and cause goiter.

What You Need To Know: Goitrogens are naturally occurring substances that can interfere with the thyroid gland's ability to uptake and utilize iodine. The thyroid needs iodine to produce the two main thyroid hormones, T3 and T4, which are involved in the regulation of many biological functions, including:

- Metabolism
- Body temperature
- Mood and excitability
- Pulse and heart rate
- Digestion

Goitrogens get their name from the term "goiter" which means enlargement of the thyroid gland. When the thyroid has insufficient levels of the trace mineral iodine, this can cause it to swell or enlarge in an attempt to absorb more iodine.

When this happens, a person may experience symptoms, such as:

A lump below the Adam's apple	Tightness in the throat	Scratchy throat
Swollen neck veins	Depression	Weight gain
Hair loss	Brain fog	Sensitivity to cold
Low energy	Fatigue	Poor memory

If someone has been diagnosed with hypothyroidism <u>due to iodine deficiency</u>, then cruciferous vegetables may not be appropriate for that person to eat until they correct their iodine status and regain the normal function of their thyroid.

However, when there *is* sufficient iodine in a person's body, goitrogenic foods should have no negative effects on thyroid function. In fact, goitrogenic compounds are widely recognized as being exceptionally health-promoting.

For example, the isothiocyanate compounds in cruciferous vegetables are well known for their powerful anti-cancer and antioxidant properties. Nevertheless, isothiocyanates are goitrogenic. So, is the answer to forgo consuming these health-enhancing nutrients? No, we just need to maintain healthy iodine levels in the body so our thyroid can do its job and we can continue to eat an abundance of healthy plants - including cruciferous leafy greens!

Many whole plant foods contain small amounts of iodine, though the amount in each food depends on the levels of iodine in the soil or water from which it came. Some of these sources include:

Asparagus	Green beans	Mushrooms	Spinach
Spring greens	Watercress	Strawberries	Potatoes
Cranberries	Prunes	Corn	Kale
Nori	Wakame	Dulce	Whole grains

Sea vegetables are the richest plant sources of iodine. Including small amounts of sea vegetables, like dulce, nori, or wakame, once or twice per week can help to ensure adequate iodine levels.

The recommended daily intake of iodine is 150 mcg per day. If you are experiencing symptoms of iodine deficiency, consider having your levels tested and making dietary adjustments if needed.

Halogens

In today's polluted environment, goitrogen exposure is much more common than you might think. Iodine belongs to a family of elements known as halogens, utilized extensively throughout various industries. The goitrogenic and endocrine-disrupting effects of these compounds are well known. Yet, rather than calling for a stop to the chemical poisoning of the public, the industry-funded media would rather convince you to be afraid of your kale salad.

Elements within the halogen family include:

- Iodine
- Astatine

- Bromine
- Chlorine
- Fluorine

The three halogens of most concern when it comes to goitrogenic effects are **bromine**, **chlorine**, and **fluorine**. These elements are similar in structure to iodine, so they can bind to iodine receptors on the thyroid and block or reduce its ability to produce T3 and T4.

The widespread industrial use of these compounds makes it virtually impossible to avoid coming in contact with at least one of them on a daily basis. However, there are steps we can take to limit our exposure.

Bromine

Bromine, in its industrial forms, has no biological value in the human body and should be avoided as much as possible. Exposure to bromine can come from a wide range of sources:

- Disinfectants in pools, hot tubs, and spas.
- Fumigants (pesticides) for agricultural crops, termites, and other residential pests.
- Some asthma inhaler medications.
- Added to baked goods to improve the elasticity of the dough. In many countries, bromine is banned as a food additive.
- Brominated vegetable oils are emulsifiers in soft drinks and other beverages.
- Added to cosmetics and fragrances.
- Contaminated drinking water.
- Brominated flame-retardants are found in many consumer products, such as plastics, foams, upholstery, mattresses, carpets, curtains, fabric blinds, computers, laptops, phones, televisions, household appliances, wires,

electrical cables, insulation materials, automobile seat covers and fillings, bumpers, overhead compartments, and other parts of automobiles, airplanes, and trains.
- Hundreds of thousands of metric tons of brominated flame-retardants are produced every year and continue to accumulate in the environment.
- Bromine is absorbed through the skin, lungs, and intestines.

Bromine toxicity can cause apathy, depression, headaches, irritability, endocrine disruption, immune system impairment, reproductive toxicity, cancer, adverse effects on fetal and child development, and damage to neurologic function.

Although bromine is virtually ubiquitous in our society, there are steps you can take to reduce your exposure:

1. Eat organic produce. Brominated fumigants are not permitted in organic agriculture.
2. Avoid consuming anything out of a plastic container.
3. If you have a hot tub or sauna, install an ozone purification system. These devices can keep the water clean and minimize contamination from bromine.
4. Avoid the use of synthetic cosmetics, perfumes, and other fragrances.
5. Avoid consuming commercial baked goods and processed foods.
6. Use indoor air purifiers or keep good ventilation in your home by opening windows.
7. Use a shower filter. See the *Recommended Products* section at the back of this book for the filter I use.
8. Invest in a quality water distiller. See the *Recommended Products and Tools* section at the back of this book for a discount code on the distillers I use.

Chlorine

If you frequently swim in chlorinated swimming pools or drink chlorinated tap water, then your thyroid is likely being compromised. Chlorine, as well as chloramine (chlorine + ammonia), are commonly added to water as disinfectants against bacteria, parasites, molds, and algae. While they may effectively kill pathogenic bacteria, they also produce toxic chemicals known as disinfectant byproducts (DBPs) that are known to cause cancer, endocrine disruption, birth defects, and more.

With all of that in mind, chlorine, chloramine, and their DBPs can also negatively impact beneficial probiotics in the gut, contributing to dysbiosis and disrupting what is known as the gut-thyroid connection.

A robust population of beneficial gut bacteria is needed for the proper absorption of essential minerals (copper, iodine, iron, selenium, zinc) that are required in the synthesis and utilization of thyroid hormones. In fact, about 20 percent of the conversion from inactive T4 into active T3 is carried out directly by probiotic bacteria in the gut!

When the gut is in a state of dysbiosis, bacterial endotoxins called lipopolysaccharide (LPS) are able to leak through the gut wall and create systemic inflammation throughout the body. LPS has been shown to decrease levels of thyroid hormones by inhibiting the conversion of inactive T4 into active T3. Additionally, LPS reduces thyroid hormone receptor expression (known as "reverse T3"), so when T3 binds to cell receptor sites, it doesn't initiate the intended response - like a key that fits into a lock but won't turn.

In addition to swimming pools, hot tubs, and drinking water, chlorine bleach is used in the whitening process of toilet paper, tissue paper, and other products. In the production of these bleached products, chemicals such as dioxins can form, which are known to cause thyroid disruption. Many people are exposing their delicate membranes (anus and nasal mucosa) to these chemicals on a daily basis, which may be affecting their thyroid function.

Perchlorate

Perchlorate is a naturally occurring, as well as man-made synthetic chlorine-based compound.

Synthetic perchlorate is used in the manufacturing of rocket fuel, ammunition, explosives, flares, and fireworks. It is highly soluble in water and can persist in the environment.

Perchlorate is especially toxic and disruptive to the production of thyroid hormones.

The Colorado River is known to be heavily contaminated with perchlorate due to military and aerospace related activities. Water from the Colorado River is used to irrigate 15% of the nation's farmland, which produces 90% of the nation's winter vegetables.

There are steps we take to reduce our exposure to chlorine, chloramine, and other chlorine-containing chemicals:

1. Use a shower filter that removes chlorine and chloramine. See the *Recommended Products* section at the back of this book for the filter I use.
2. Avoid chlorinated pools and hot tubs. Look for saltwater pools and hot tubs when possible.

3. Use a home water distiller to purify your water from chlorine, chloramine, and countless other chemicals found in tap water. See the *Recommended Products* section at the back of this book for a discount code on the distillers I use.
4. Buy from your local farmer's markets where they are less likely to spray leafy greens and other vegetables with chlorinated sanitizer solutions.
5. Grow your own microgreens, sprouts, and other vegetables as much as you can.
6. Get serious about learning to grow at least some of your own food - industrialized agriculture (both organic and conventional) have a variety of issues.

Fluoride

Fluoride is a naturally occurring mineral found in the environment. Most people know of fluoride as a wonderful addition to drinking water and dental products for the prevention of cavities.

In 1945, Grand Rapids, Michigan was the first city in the United States to fluoridate its public water supply. By 2008, more than 72% of the nation's public water supply was receiving fluoridation.

Health officials and government agencies claim that water fluoridation is a safe and effective method for preventing dental cavities despite the fact that there is no discernible difference in tooth decay between the countries that fluoridate their water and those that do not.

It seems rather disingenuous that the U.S. government would be so altruistic regarding your dental health, while at the same time, they have allowed tobacco, candy, soda, processed meats, and junk food to be marketed to our youth. They drag their feet when it comes to removing, banning, or preventing toxic chemicals from being used in consumer products that make people sick and pollute our environment. Yet, when it comes to getting fluoride on your teeth, the government is apparently on the ball.

When you look a little closer, you will find that the fluoride being added to water supplies is not the naturally occurring fluoride from the soil. The type of fluoride used by your local water treatment facility is most likely fluorosilicic acid, which is a corrosive industrial waste product captured in the air pollution control devices of the phosphate fertilizer industry.

Back in the 1950s and 60s, farms and communities located near these industry facilities were having their crops and livestock harmed or killed from exposure to the toxic fluoride gasses and particulates being released. The U.S. Department of Agriculture has cited airborne fluoride for causing more worldwide damage to domestic animals than any other air pollutant.

The industry was then required to capture the waste but it was expensive and difficult to dispose of, so it was allowed to be packaged and sold to communities for the purpose of water fluoridation.

Studies have linked fluoride to reduced IQ, neurotoxicity, cancer, gastrointestinal dysbiosis, dental fluorosis, skeletal fluorosis, bone fractures, reduced nitric oxide, and thyroid disruption. In fact, fluoride was used to treat hyperthyroidism up until the 1950s, prior to the development of other thyroid-suppressing medications. The goitrogenic effects of fluoride are due to its ability to compete with iodine for uptake by receptors in the thyroid and cells throughout the body.

Common sources of fluoride intake include:

- Drinking water
- Toothpaste
- Commercial beverages
- Tea
- Processed foods
- Processed meats
- Pesticides
- Dental products
- Pharmaceuticals drugs
- Teflon pans
- Industrial workplace exposure

Since there are so many potential sources of exposure to fluoride, it is impossible to know how much fluoride each person is consuming. This makes it even more dangerous to mass-medicate the population - not to mention it is a violation of the Nuremberg Code to medicate someone without informed consent.

Steps you can take to reduce your exposure to unnatural sources of fluoride include:

1. Distill your water.
2. Use fluoride-free toothpaste.
3. Decline fluoride dental treatments and products.
4. Avoid processed beverages and foods.
5. Avoid non-stick cookware.
6. Buy organic produce.
7. Avoid unnecessary use of pharmaceutical drugs.

Bacterial Contamination

Claim: Eating leafy greens puts you at a higher risk of foodborne illness due to bacterial contamination.

What You Need To Know: Every few years, news reports warn us how dangerous it is to eat leafy greens because of bacterial contamination. E.coli, listeria, campylobacter, and salmonella are common strains involved in food poisoning cases.

There is no question that bacterial contamination can be a risk with any food, including leafy greens. However, the idea pushed by some organizations that eating greens is somehow more dangerous than eating bacteria-laden dead animal body parts and animal secretions is a head-scratcher. Even when these items are thoroughly cooked, they still necessitate the growth of pathogenic bacteria to break them down in the gut.

Eating a diet rich in raw plants, like leafy greens, is what creates a healthy terrain of protective gut bacteria that make someone less likely to get sick from contaminated foods in the first place! Robust populations of beneficial probiotics in the gut prevent the overgrowth of pathogenic bacteria by competing for nutrients and attachment sites to the mucus membranes of the gut.

Now, it is true that we have an agricultural system that chooses to grow many crops in sewage sludge and raw animal manure, so that does pose a definite health risk. Virtually all of the bacterial contamination that leafy greens and other vegetables are vilified for, come from cross-contamination with animal products or animal waste either in the field or during the handling and processing of the vegetables.

Additionally, the water used to irrigate most of the winter crops grown on large-scale farms in the southwest United States comes from the heavily polluted Colorado River. This accounts for roughly 90 percent of the winter crops available in the U.S.

So, yes, there are problems with the food system that impacts many of our healthiest foods, including greens. However, this does not mean that leafy greens should be avoided or eliminated from a person's diet. All that it means is that we should take the necessary precautions and work towards solutions that will allow us to eat the highest quality, cleanest leafy greens possible.

Some steps we can take to reduce our risk of foodborne illness from bacterial contamination:

1. Strengthen the gut microbiome and immune system by eating a whole food plant-exclusive diet. I believe this is the most important factor.
2. Start growing a portion of your own greens so you control the growing and handling conditions. Start small with sprouts, microgreens, or herbs and progress from there.
3. Eat organic produce as much as possible to avoid eating food grown in sewer sludge.
4. Source your greens from trusted local growers and suppliers.
5. Buy individual heads or bunches of greens instead of boxed and precut-bagged varieties, when possible. The more handling and processing the greens go through, the more chance for contamination.
6. Soak the greens in water and baking soda for 15 minutes and then rinse them thoroughly before preparing.

7. Always store greens away from any animal products (if you're still transitioning to a vegan diet) in your shopping cart, grocery bags, and refrigerator.

Personally, I have been eating more than a pound of leafy greens (mostly store-bought) daily for more than 12 years without any problems. I have never taken any extraordinary measures to clean my produce, though the more I learn about the food system, the more it seems like a good idea when buying from grocery stores.

When it comes down to it, each person must make their own decisions about what they choose to eat and what food safety measures they feel are necessary.

Anti-Nutrients

Claim: You will develop nutritional deficiencies by eating a plant-based diet because plants contain anti-nutrients!

What You Need To Know: "Anti-nutrients" are phytochemicals in certain foods that appear to inhibit the bioavailability and absorption rates of certain nutrients. Whether we're talking about alkaloids, lectins, tannins, oxalates, goitrogens, phytates, phytoestrogens, or any other "anti-nutrient," - context matters.

The majority of the research done on specific "anti-nutrients" is conducted using the isolated compound, which is either given in unnaturally high doses to animals or administered to cells in a petri dish. Besides the fact that these are mainly non-human studies, they are done in a context of exposure that we would never consume at one time. It is well understood that compounds in isolation often have very different effects than when consumed in whole foods containing an array of cofactors, enzymes, vitamins, minerals, fiber, and other phytochemicals.

What we know is that diets rich in whole plant foods, including those containing anti-nutrients, are associated with less inflammation, lower chronic disease risk, and fewer - *not more* - nutritional deficiencies than omnivorous diets. It seems the most common deficiencies one might expect from a whole-food, plant-exclusive diet is deficiencies of cancer, heart disease, diabetes, kidney stones, heavy metals, and industrial toxins.

Unfortunately, what tends to get hoisted into the headlines are either sensationalized findings from industry-funded studies that make people feel good about their bad habits, or questionable assumptions made from extreme cases. Such was the case when an 88-year-old woman ate roughly three pounds of bok choy every day for several months and ended up in a coma due to severe hypothyroidism. Nearly every major news outlet took the opportunity to warn their viewers about the dangers of eating too many vegetables - because that's clearly a problem in today's world (#sarcasm).

The good news is that when these foods are eaten in a balanced manner, the so-called "anti-nutrients" are actually beneficial in many ways.

Anti-Nutrients Are Hormetic

As I mentioned earlier in this chapter, hormesis occurs when mild stress induces beneficial cellular adaptations. The small amount of stress caused by many of these natural plant compounds trains and educates our cells and immune system to be more resilient when challenged.

Similarly, crops grown outdoors in the elements (wind, rain, drought, insects, etc.) tend to have higher concentrations of some of these "anti-nutrient" compounds. The mild stress from insects and weather imparts a hormetic effect on the plants, encouraging stronger root systems, increased phytonutrient production, drought resistance, and stronger immune systems.

So, eating plants that contain stress-induced compounds which helped them survive harsh conditions, in turn, helps to strengthen the survival skills of our own cells. Isn't it amazing how nature works!? For example, in greens like kale, polyphenol compounds such as tannins provide protection against mold, fungi, and insects. Tannins are known to reduce dietary iron absorption, but they are also believed to protect against conditions like oxidative stress, cardiovascular disease, cancer, and osteoporosis.

Man-made toxins (pesticides, food additives, industrial chemicals, etc.) on the other hand, create a stress response in our cells that results in toxicity, mutation, and death. These are the types of toxins that present a real danger to the health of humans, animals, and our environment.

Anti-Nutrients Are Nutrients

When we look at "anti-nutrients" from a holistic viewpoint, we see that they are, in fact, nutrients. These compounds work synergistically within the complex matrix of whole plant foods to provide an overall benefit to the human body.

Many of these nutrients have qualities that are prebiotic, antioxidant, anti-inflammatory, anti-carcinogenic, and cardiovascular protective. Many of the foods that contain these compounds are known for their health-promoting qualities. I recommend reading the book, *Whole*, by T. Colin

Campbell Ph.D. to learn more about the importance of looking at foods holistically, rather than through the context of isolated nutrients.

With that said, there is the possibility for specific circumstances that may require a person to avoid certain plant compounds at certain times. Someone with iron deficiency anemia may want to limit their ingestion of tannins and phytates, someone with kidney disease may want to limit their exposure to oxalates, and someone with a severe iodine deficiency may want to avoid goitrogens until the underlying cause of these health conditions is healed.

For relatively healthy individuals, though - eating foods that contain "anti-nutrients" in normal dietary amounts and as part of a balanced plant-based diet, will only add to their healthy nutrient profile. Here are a few additional ways to reduce the already small chance of consuming too many of these specific "anti-nutrients":

1. Eat whole plant foods - preferably organic.
2. Avoid unnecessary supplementation, and when supplementing, use whole-food-based supplements.
3. Eat a wide variety of plants.
4. Rotate the varieties of plants that you eat throughout each month to avoid the slight chance of accumulating excess "anti-nutrients."
5. Soak, rinse, and sprout nuts, seeds, lentils, and beans.
6. If desired, use wet heat (boiling, steaming, pressure cooking) to minimally heat-process anti-nutrient-containing foods.
7. Stay hydrated.
8. Maintain a healthy gut microbiome.

5

The Proof Is In The Salad Bowl

They say if you want to be successful at something, study those that have been successful doing it. That is exactly what I did back in 2011 when I stumbled into the plant-based world. I was very intentional about whom I took advice from. I wanted to learn from those who had been successfully eating a whole food, plant-based diet for many years and who exuded the level of health that I desired.

I quickly noticed a common thread among nearly every healthy, long-term, plant-based practitioner - they consumed a significant amount of leafy greens and followed a balanced dietary approach. When I compared their long-term results to those of people who promoted more extreme and unbalanced approaches, let's just say, the proof is in the salad bowl.

The goal is not to follow anyone's diet exactly but to look at what is working for successful people and take the key points that resonate with you to use in your own diet and lifestyle.

In this chapter, I want to highlight some of the people that helped me understand the importance of making leafy greens a substantial part of my diet. I call them my "Green Team".

My Green Team

Tanny Raw

21+ years whole food plant-based vegan
16+ years raw vegan
TannyRaw on YouTube

Tanny grew up in South Carolina eating the standard American diet of macaroni and cheese, hotdogs, hamburgers, french fries, eggs, sausage, grilled cheese, beef liver, grits, biscuits with gravy, breakfast cereals, whole milk, etc. As she got older, she developed various health conditions including irritable bowel syndrome (IBS), leaky gut, constipation, nodular acne, depression, lupus, brain fog, weight gain, and debilitating arthritis.

When doctors only had drugs to offer her, Tanny started doing her own research and eventually found the whole food, plant-based lifestyle. For the next five years, she ate a whole-food, plant-based diet, consisting of predominantly cooked meals. This way of eating did provide some improvements in her health conditions. Still, it wasn't until she transitioned to a low-fat, high-carb, raw vegan diet and incorporated fasting and cleansing, that she experienced the level of healing that she was searching for. In less than a year, Tanny lost over 75 pounds and regained so much energy that she says the people around her have a hard time keeping up with her.

Tanny credits leafy greens as one of the most important factors in her health transformation and success on a raw vegan diet. She says that greens are what brought her from death to life and she eats well over one pound of leafy greens every day.

Dan McDonald (The Life Regenerator)

22+ years raw vegan
regenerateyourlife.org

Dan McDonald grew up on the West Coast where he was raised on a standard American diet. From a young age, Dan was using drugs and drinking alcohol. At 19, Dan became interested in lifting weights, which led him to eat a high-protein diet with large amounts of chicken, steak, and eggs.

Around this time, Dan received a Champion juicer from his parents which he used to make daily freshly pressed juices. Even though he was exercising and drinking vegetable juices, Dan continued to struggle off and on with drugs, alcohol, and low self-worth until he discovered the power of raw, living foods in October of 2000.

Through raw foods, fasting, deep introspection, and spiritual work, Dan overcame his addictions to drugs and alcohol and has turned his life's struggle into inspiration for countless people around the world.

Dan has inspired thousands to embrace a living food lifestyle that includes fruits, vegetables, herbs, leafy greens, nuts, seeds, and connecting with your higher power.

Many years ago, Dan explained in a YouTube video that he focuses on hydration and fruits in the first part of the day, and in the evening, he enjoys a big salad as a "celebration of life." I connected with that philosophy and have maintained a similar approach to this day.

John Kohler

27+ years raw vegan
Growing Your Greens on YouTube
discountjuicers.com

John Kohler is another West Coast raw foodist who has built up one of the most popular gardening channels on YouTube called Growing Your Greens. John grew up eating a standard American diet and suffered from asthma, allergies, and eczema. Shortly after graduating from college, John nearly lost his life when he was diagnosed with spinal meningitis and complement immune deficiency. His doctors told him there was no treatment for his condition and that he might not make it out of the hospital alive. John did make it out of the hospital thanks to what he says was an act from higher powers.

John was then determined to learn how to strengthen his immune system and came across a television commercial by Jay Kordich (The Juiceman) talking about the power of juicing and raw food for boosting immunity. He picked up a juicer and began juicing as much organic produce as he could. Six months later at a health food store, John found a book called, Cleanse and Purify Thyself, by Dr. Richard

Anderson, explaining colon cleaning and raw foods. John completed a colon cleanse and started eating raw foods in addition to juicing and his eczema cleared up for the first time in his life.

From that point on, John committed to eating raw foods and continued his research into diet and nutrition. He says after about ten years, he realized how important the quality of the food we eat is, and so he began learning to grow a garden. He has now taught (and continues to teach) hundreds of thousands of people how to improve their health by living a healthy lifestyle, gardening, and eating more raw foods - with a strong emphasis on getting in at least 1-2 pounds of leafy greens daily!

Dr. Fred Bisci

58+ years raw vegan
Author of *Your Healthy Journey*

Dr. Bisci has a fascinating and inspiring story. He grew up in New York City in the 1930s and struggled with dyslexia and a speech impediment as a child, which impacted his confidence and self-image. His family didn't have much money, so he says he never overindulged in high-protein animal foods.

He avoided school as much as possible because he didn't think he was smart and didn't want others to find out. He instead focused his attention on athletics, including boxing and weightlifting, and later joined the Navy. While in the Navy, Fred had a conversation with one of the boxing coaches, who suggested that he take a closer look at his nutrition and what he was putting into his body. Fred took the man's advice and when he got out of the Navy, he met a Natural Hygienist who introduced him to a raw vegan dietary approach and water fasting.

Fred began studying with many European health practitioners who taught him more about water fasting, eating sprouts, and raw foods. Fred put this knowledge into practice in his own life as he continued with his athletic pursuits. Due to a shoulder injury that he sustained in a car accident, Fred transitioned from weightlifting to long-distance running. Throughout this time, Fred never deviated from his raw vegan diet, which was comprised of a lot of salads, sprouts, juices, smoothies, and a moderate amount of fruit, nuts, seeds, and avocados.

Fred started to notice during marathons and while training 50-70 miles per week, he was running out of stamina mid-way through his runs. He discovered he was not eating enough fruit to sustain his level of activity and once he added more fruit to his diet, he was easily able to complete a 20-mile run with no problems.

Through his athletic accomplishments, working with people as a Clinical Nutritionist for more than 40 years, and all of the experience he has accumulated throughout his 93 years (and counting) of life, Fred encourages a balanced approach to diet and life in general. He says that we should not overeat any one type of food. He recommends eating a healthy mixture of leafy greens, sprouts, fruits, nuts, and seeds in combination with clean water, fresh air, sunlight, physical activity, periodic cleansing, spirituality, and healthy relationships.

Dr. Bisci is a blessing to everyone he meets. He is a shining example of how to overcome adversity and live a life of purpose with wisdom, strength, humbleness, faith, service, compassion, love, longevity, and health.

Dr. Caldwell Esselstyn, Jr., M.D.

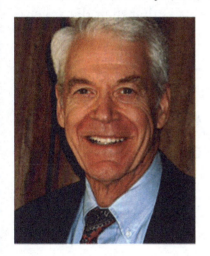

39+ years whole food plant-based
Author of *Prevent and Reverse Heart Disease*
dresselstyn.com

Dr. Caldwell Esselstyn Jr. is a giant in the whole food plant-based world as well as in the field of Cardiology and lifestyle medicine. Dr. Esselstyn grew up on a beef and dairy farm in New York and from a dietary standpoint, he says he was a "cholesterol-aholic."

Dr. Esselstyn graduated from Yale University in 1956 and also won a gold medal as a member of the American rowing team in the 1956 Summer Olympics. He earned his medical degree from Western Reserve University in 1961. In 1968, Dr. Esselstyn received a Bronze Star for his service as an Army surgeon in Vietnam.

Dr. Esselstyn and his wife, Ann, switched to a whole food plant-based diet in 1984 after Dr. Esselstyn's research revealed to him that various cultures around the world had heart disease and cancer rates that were dramatically less frequent than the United States - in some cultures it was virtually non-existent. He found that the common denominator in all of these cultures was that their diets were whole food, plant-based, with no dietary oil.

In 1985, Dr. Esselstyn went to his Department of Cardiology and asked for 24 patients to enroll in a study to see what results could be achieved by having these heart disease patients adopt a whole food, plant-based dietary approach. Within months of following Dr. Esselstyn's program, all of the patients that followed the protocol experience dramatic improvements in their angina symptoms, lower cholesterol, and improvement in blood flow to their hearts. When Dr. Esselstyn followed up with these patients twenty years later, they remained symptom-free.

One of my students who frequently attends the raw food classes that I teach in Minnesota learned of Dr. Esselstyn through one of my presentations. This gentleman had been suffering from heart disease, so I suggested that he try reaching out to Dr. Esselstyn for a second opinion regarding the treatment he had been receiving. The next time I saw him in class he let me know that he had received a phone call from Dr. Esselstyn himself and they had a great conversation. Several months later I saw him again in class and he let me know that his heart disease was reversing using Dr. Esselstyn's dietary approach!

Dr. Esselstyn recommends a low-fat, whole-food, plant-based diet, including at least six fist-sized portions of leafy greens per day and no added oils. He and his wife are great ambassadors for the longevity-promoting qualities of a diet rich in leafy green vegetables.

Dr. T. Colin Campbell

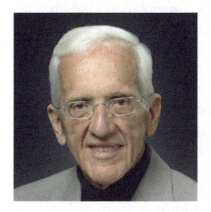

33+ years whole food plant-based
Author of *The China Study*
nutritionstudies.org

Dr. Campbell is known as the father of the whole food, plant-based diet - as he was the first to coin the phrase. Coincidently, he grew up on a dairy farm in the United States and had high esteem for animal protein throughout his early life.

He started his education by getting a B.S. in pre-veterinary medicine but changed paths and went on to earn his M.S. in nutrition and biochemistry in 1958 and his Ph.D. in nutrition, biochemistry, and microbiology in 1961 from Cornell University.

After graduate school, Dr. Campbell worked at MIT for three years where he was trained in toxicological biochemistry. He then went to work at Virginia Tech where he was asked to coordinate a project in the Philippines to help feed malnourished children.

It was through this work in the Philippines that Dr. Campbell discovered the carcinogenicity and dangers of animal protein. Liver cancer was of interest to researchers in the Philippines and Dr. Campbell observed that the children who came from the few families that could afford to eat "the best" diets - meaning those that contained animal protein - were at the highest risk of developing liver cancer. When he returned to the United States, he received a grant from the National Institutes of Health (NIH) to continue his research.

Over the next few decades, Dr. Campbell's research team repeatedly found that they could essentially "turn on" and "turn off" cancer cells just by feeding them casein - the main protein in cow's milk. This was in complete opposition to what he believed about animal protein growing up on a dairy farm; however, it supported his observations of the children in the Philippines.

Dr. Campbell then had an opportunity to work on a project in China to study cancer rates throughout various Chinese communities. The data that was collected from this project was consistent with the results of his team's research and would eventually become the impetus for Dr. Campbell to write what would turn out to be one of the most influential nutrition books ever written. That book is The China Study, which has sold well over a million copies and has been the catalyst for a seismic shift in the public perception regarding animal protein and human health. Since that time Dr. Campbell has written two more excellent books, called "Whole" and "The Future of Nutrition."

Leafy greens have been a staple in Dr. Campbell's whole food plant-based diet since 1990, and at the current age of 89, his body, mind, and spirit are a testament to this dietary approach. When asked about the role leafy greens should play in a person's diet, Dr. Campbell says, "Eat as much of them as you can - they are excellent foods."

Dr. Ann Wigmore

35+ years whole food plant-based
Author of *The Hippocrates Diet and Health Program*
annwigmore.org

Dr. Ann Wigmore was born in Lithuania in 1909. She was raised by her grandmother, who was a natural doctor that cared for wounded soldiers during wartime. Ann witnessed soldiers recover from their injuries and illnesses with the help of herbs, grasses, and weeds that her grandmother collected.

This experience would have a profound influence on her later in life.

As a child, Ann struggled with her health and after moving to the United States to live with her parents when she was 16 years old, she began eating like an American, which added to her health issues. At the age of 50, she was diagnosed with colon cancer and told she had six months to live.

Rather than using conventional treatments, Ann followed the example set by her grandmother and looked to nature and God for answers. She began consuming raw greens, sprouted blended seeds, and cultured grains. Ann was able to completely heal her body naturally, and from this experience, she felt called to open a healing center.

Before opening the center, Ann dedicated herself to studying naturopathy and homeopathy and eventually obtained a Doctor of Divinity degree from an American college. In 1963, she opened America's first holistic health center, the Hippocrates Health Institute, in Boston, Massachusetts where she taught her students what she called "The Living Foods Lifestyle" program.

The "Living Foods Lifestyle" teaches people how to grow, prepare, and eat whole plant foods - emphasizing leafy greens, microgreens, and wheatgrass. The program also covers movement, yoga, meditation, positive effects of nature, cleansing techniques, and connection to one's spirituality, all in ways that would support restorative healing.

Twenty-seven years later, in 1990, Ann opened another center called Ann Wigmore Natural Health Institute in Puerto Rico. People from all over the world stay at the center and learn to awaken their innate power to heal and live naturally.

Ann believed, "There are no incurable diseases if one lives in harmony with nature."

Dr. Wigmore passed away in 1994 due to a fire, but her mission is carried on through the healing centers that she created.

6

Stumbling Over Salads

Why People Struggle To Eat Greens

If salads are so great for our health and longevity, why do so many people have a hard time enjoying greens? There are many possible explanations for this, but I believe a fundamental factor is that our palates have been corrupted from living in a state of constant stimulation.

From the day most American babies are conceived they gestate on the hyper-stimulating diet of their mothers. Once born, many babies are given formula and baby foods that contain added sugars, oils, and chemical additives. Throughout childhood, they are given sugary cereals, birthday cakes, pizza, ice cream, donuts, cookies, pies, soda, candy, fast food, etc. Even when they are given fruits and vegetables, they are often covered in a sugary syrup or dipped into a fatty, salty dressing.

We have conditioned our taste buds and gut microbiome to desire a constant level of hyper-stimulation that no natural food can compete with. The high caloric density, chemical flavorings, and strategically designed mouth feel of processed foods trigger an exaggerated dopamine (pleasure) response in our brain that the food industry calls the "bliss point." The bliss point creates a biochemical addiction to these foods that keeps people coming back for more.

Furthermore, processed foods are not devised with just one bliss point. Rather, they combine multiple ingredients - each having its own bliss point. These foods have just the right amount of sweetness, saltiness, creaminess, and mouth feel that individually and collectively create the maximum amount of dopamine stimulation.

Having multiple bliss points allows these products to elude triggering what is known as sensory-specific satiety, which describes the gradual decline of satisfaction that we get while eating one flavor or food. For example, you might decline a second helping of your savory dinner because you feel full, but when a sweet dessert is offered, you suddenly have an appetite again.

The human body was never designed to encounter the hyper-stimulating foods that we are exposed to today. According to foodtank.com, 73% of the United States food supply is ultra-processed food!

A 2019 study titled "Characterizing Ultra-Processed Foods by Energy Density, Nutrient Density, and Cost" found that more than 60% of the average American's calories are coming from these manufactured foods. Consuming these products causes our baseline dopamine response to be set at an artificially high level, making anything less stimulating seem bland, boring, or flavorless.

DIETARY DOPAMINE RESPONSE SPECTRUM

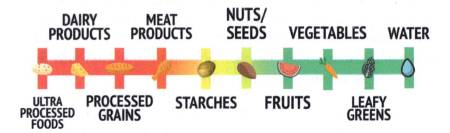

The Dietary Dopamine Response Spectrum depicted above illustrates how different kinds of foods elicit varying levels of dopamine production from the body when consumed. The further to the left of the spectrum you go, the more exaggerated the food's bliss point and addictive qualities become.

Foods within the green and yellow segments of the spectrum create a dopamine response that falls within the body's normal and healthy limits. If you eat within these parameters, you will derive an appropriate level of enjoyment and satisfaction from the foods you eat. The person who eats within the yellow and green segments of the spectrum will be much more likely to have a healthy relationship with food.

As you move into the red segment, you encounter foods that create a hyper-stimulation of the dopamine response. The various bliss points that many of these foods trigger in the brain overwhelm the system and eventually desensitize the dopamine receptors. This leads people to eat compulsively and to develop unhealthy, addictive relationships (cravings, withdrawals, binging, etc.) with food.

As the dopamine response system becomes desensitized, we require increasing amounts of stimulation in order to obtain the same feelings of satisfaction - just like with addictive drugs. We are driven to eat more and more hyper-stimulating foods to feel that "food high."

This explains why so many people find fresh fruits, vegetables, and leafy greens to be unappealing. The bliss point and caloric density of fruits and vegetables are magnitudes lower than those in processed foods.

Leafy greens, in particular, have the lowest caloric density of any plant foods, meaning they are likely to generate the lowest dopamine response in the brain. No wonder the average person considers eating salad to be cruel and unusual punishment!

To compound this issue, people lack the understanding of how to put together a healthy, filling, and delicious salad - making their experience even more miserable. However, I'm going to teach you how to optimize the bliss points within your salad that will turn any salad into a bowl of culinary euphoria!

Before we do that, let's first make sure you're not committing these six common salad-making mistakes that will sabotage your salad experience.

Common Salad Mistakes To Avoid

Mistake #1: Too Few Calories

The most common cause of an unsatisfying salad is a lack of volume and calories. Most people have been conditioned to believe that a serving of salad fits on a plate. If you can fit your entire salad on a plate, you had better read the rest of this book sitting down. Even if you are privy enough to eat your salad out of a bowl - if people don't confuse your personal bowl of salad for what is being passed around for everyone to share, then you've got some work to do.

As we've covered, greens are packed full of nutrition, yet they are extremely low in caloric density. In general, I'm not one to recommend counting calories, but it is helpful to have a ballpark idea of how many calories you're eating throughout the day - especially if you're not feeling satisfied.

I am not suggesting that we should be getting the majority of our calories from greens, but depending on which greens we use in our salads, it can make a big difference in how full we feel after the meal.

The list below illustrates the approximate number of calories in various salad greens:

Salad Greens	Calories Per 100 Grams	Calories Per Pound
Bok choy	13	59
Iceberg lettuce	14	63
Green leaf lettuce	15	68
Romaine lettuce	17	77
Spinach	23	104
Arugula	25	113
Green cabbage	25	113
Red cabbage	31	140
Collards	32	144
Kale	35	158

As you can see, when it comes to calories, all leaves are not created equally.

If you have trouble feeling full after your salads, then consider including some of the more hearty greens, like kale, collards, arugula, or cabbage. Also, be sure to include plenty of filling vegetables, sprouts, and other toppings to help increase the overall caloric load of the salad.

Most people are lucky if they've got 6 oz of greens in their salad. What I am suggesting is using a *minimum* of one pound (16 oz) of leafy greens in your salad! This not only gives you more valuable nutrients from the greens but also gives you a larger volume of salad to fill with more vegetables and roughage to fill up your stomach.

Mistake #2: Poorly Prepared Ingredients

The second mistake I see people making is haphazardly rough chopping a few ingredients, throwing them into a bowl, and calling it a salad. This is a sure way to create a less-than-spectacular salad.

There is nothing worse than big chunky salads that are awkward to chew. It not only makes the salad difficult and uncomfortable to chew, but you get fewer ingredients in each bite. Finely chopping and shredding your ingredients will allow them to combine better in the salad and allow you to get more flavor on each forkful of food.

In fact, the way we chop or cut our fruits and vegetables literally changes the way they feel and taste in our mouths. For example, a tomato cut in wedges tastes different than a thinly sliced tomato. Chopped carrots taste different than shredded carrots. And finely chopped kale is a completely different experience than when it is roughly chopped.

Even boxed salad greens become more palatable when they are given a few good chops before going into the salad bowl. A common complaint I hear is that salads are difficult to eat. Learning to properly chop, dice, slice, and mince your ingredients will open up a whole new salad experience for you.

Additional preparation techniques you can use to elevate your salad experience are listed below:

- Use organic and locally grown ingredients as much as possible - they are usually more flavorful. Get to know the farmers at your local farmer's market to take advantage of the high-quality produce they offer.

- Use the freshest ingredients as you can. Avoid using the wrinkly bell pepper and limp carrots that you found in the back of the fridge.

- Learn how to pick out the highest quality fruits and vegetables at the markets where you shop.

- Use homegrown ingredients to add incredible flavor and freshness to the salad. Sprouts and microgreens work great for those people that don't have space for a vegetable garden.

- Purchase loose heads/bunches of greens rather than pre-washed/packaged greens when possible.

You will be surprised at how much of a difference it makes when you put a little extra time and energy into selecting and preparing your salad ingredients.

Mistake #3: Inadequate Equipment

I cannot help but cringe when I see someone preparing a salad with the wrong equipment. If you are serious about eating more leafy greens, then you need to invest in the tools that will make the process of creating salads more enjoyable.

Often when I stay with friends or family, and we make our dinner salads, we end up preparing the ingredients on tiny cutting boards with tiny knives. This increases the preparation time and makes the process more tedious, which puts another unnecessary barrier between people and more leafy greens.

Having inadequate kitchen tools to prepare food is like trying to run a marathon in snow boots. You could do it, but it would be an unpleasant experience, and it would take you much longer to complete the process. If you only ever ran in snow boots, you would think that running is an awful activity, and you would probably never want to do it. However, if you were to purchase a nice pair of running shoes that fit well and were comfortable, you would likely be much more inclined to go running. The same can be said of preparing salads or any other meals. The right tools will set you up for success.

I have listed all of the products that I use and recommend in the *Recommended Products and Tools* section.

Bowls

As I mentioned, if your bowl doesn't turn heads, it's probably too small. A real salad deserves a bowl that would commonly be used as a potluck serving dish. You will know when you've reached the right size of salad when you start getting asked, "Are you going to eat all of that?!"

I recommend finding a nice, large bowl that will fit at least two pounds of salad - roughly 12 inches or so. I prefer a good quality glass or single-block wood bowl, as they typically contain the least amount of chemicals that could potentially transfer into the food.

Many wooden and bamboo bowls are made of multiple pieces of wood that have been glued together with "food-safe" glues that have the potential to break down when exposed to hot liquids, vinegar, or alcohol.

Food-safe does not mean food-grade. In other words, it can still have harmful chemicals, like formaldehyde, that you do not want in your food.

Choose a bowl you enjoy looking at and are excited to eat from. This bowl will hold the nourishment that is used to build the cells of your body, so put some thought into it.

Once you've got your bowl, all that is left is to fill it up with delicious salad and enjoy the experience.

Knives

There are not many things worse than preparing a large salad with a small knife. Especially when your goal is to eat a large salad every day, you want a knife that will make the job as efficient and enjoyable as possible.

Get yourself a couple of large chef knives, a serrated knife, and some smaller paring knives. This way, whether you are chopping up a large head of lettuce, peeling a lemon, or slicing tomatoes, you always have the right knife for the job.

Cutting Boards

Having a cutting board that is too small might be one of the few things worse than having the wrong knives. There is something about having a big cutting board that makes preparing a meal so satisfying.

I recommend looking for a nice cutting board that is at least around 14" x 17", which is what we have had in our kitchen for many years. However, we recently upgraded to a 16" x 20" custom-made cutting board made from a single block of hard maple wood, free of petroleum-based finishes.

We wanted our cutting board to be made from a single block of wood because, like wooden bowls, most wood cutting boards are made from multiple pieces that are glued together with toxic glues that have the potential to break down. I feel that keeping wood glue and other chemicals (like microplastics, phthalates, and Bisphenols in plastic cutting boards) away from our food is the safest choice. See the *Recommended Products and Tools* section for the company that we purchased our cutting board from.

Once you have a nice, large cutting board, you will never want to prepare your food on anything else.

Quality Appliances

If it is within your budget to purchase a few high-quality kitchen appliances, they will exponentially add ease and convenience to making salads and other healthy meals.

Quality appliances may cost more upfront, but they often last decades and undoubtedly provide you with a better final product. Compared to cheaper appliances that often break down much sooner, you will be able to make recipes that look and taste more delicious.

The top 3 appliances that I recommend for making incredible salads:

1. High-speed blender (for dressings)

2. Food processor (for quick chopping and batch-prepping ingredients)

3. Water distiller (for dressings and washing produce)

See *Recommended Products and Tools* for specific products I recommend.

If these appliances are not currently in your budget, do not let this stop you from making healthy choices. We all have to do the best we can no matter the situation we are in.

I encourage you to start a savings fund to purchase these appliances in the future. It is not just an investment in an appliance; it is an investment in your health and future.

There are few things more valuable than our health. It is better to be proactive today than reactive tomorrow. Do everything you can to set yourself up for a future life of vigor and longevity.

Mistake #4: Not Enough Variety

The reason many people believe that salads are boring and bland is that they are simply making boring and bland salads. This is not an indictment against salads - it just shows the average person's lack of awareness when it comes to making amazing salads.

Variety is one of the greatest things about salads. It's like having a blank canvas and a seemingly endless selection of paints to create with. There are at least hundreds of different combinations of leafy greens, toppings, and dressings that we have to play with.

Most people use romaine or kale for every salad and habitually top it with tomato, carrot, onion, and ranch dressing. This is like having Bob Ross's artistic ability and only choosing to draw stick figures to hang on your fridge. Once you tap into your creative ability and expand your vision of what a salad can be, you start to see new ways to assemble a salad that can be just as exciting and delicious as any other meal.

I have included 17 brand-new, delicious salad dressings in the *Recipes* section at the back of this book. In the next chapter, I will teach you how to tap into your creativity and design your own salad dressings like a professional chef!

In addition to amazing dressings, here are just *a few* of the ingredients you can fill your salads with:

Apples	Apricots	Artichokes	Avocado
Beets	Beans	Berries	Broccoli
Brussels sprouts	Carrots	Cauliflower	Cucumbers
Figs	Grapes	Jackfruit	Kiwis
Leeks	Mangoes	Microgreens	Mushrooms
Nectarines	Olives	Onions	Oranges
Papaya	Pears	Peas	Peppers
Pineapple	Radishes	Raisins	Tomatoes
Sprouts	Turnips	Wild rice	Zucchini

Mistake #5: Too Much Fat

One ingredient that I do not recommend using in your salad, is oil. Nothing adds empty calories and an excessive amount of fat to a salad faster than an oily dressing.

All oils, even extra virgin olive oil, contain 120 grams of fat per tablespoon. That means just three tablespoons of oil increases the fat content of the salad by 360 calories! Often times that accounts for more than half of the total calories of the entire meal!

In addition to oil, it is not uncommon to see people load a single salad with avocado, cashew sour cream, and other nuts or seeds. This exorbitant amount of fat turns what would have been a healthy meal into a fatty, digestive quandary.

Even with all the healthy fiber and phytonutrients in a salad, adding large amounts of fat slows digestion, promotes gut dysbiosis, impairs blood flow, and can lead to constipation, fatigue, weight gain, and skin issues. *Some* healthy fat is great, but a little bit goes a long way.

Like oils, nut butters are another highly concentrated source of fat that is easy to overuse in sauces and dressings. Three cups of sesame seeds blend down into 1 cup of tahini. So, adding three tablespoons of tahini to a dressing would be like adding nine tablespoons of sesame seeds!

This is why I recommend using whole, unprocessed sources of fat in salads, dressings, and sauces. You can gauge the actual fat content much easier when you're looking at whole nuts, seeds, and avocados.

Recommended whole-food fats to use in your dressings include:

Almonds	Avocado	Brazil nuts	Cashews
Chia seeds	Flax seeds	Hazelnuts	Hemp seeds
Macadamia nuts	Pecans	Pine nuts	Pistachios
Pumpkin seeds	Sesame seeds	Sunflower seeds	Walnuts

I have found that just three tablespoons of nuts or seeds are enough to give any dressing a creamy consistency without adding excessive calories from fat. This is important because the dressing is arguably the most essential component of creating a satisfying salad.

The dressing should not be thought of as only a flavoring agent for the salad. This mindset leads people to believe a chemical-filled, oil-based product is perfectly acceptable to use as long as it tastes good. **Instead, I want you to view the dressing like any other ingredient in the salad - as a means of adding more nutrition and variety to the meal.**

We do not need to sacrifice nutrition for flavor when it comes to the dressing. The dressings in the *Recipes* section *of* this book were designed to give you the perfect blend of flavor *and* nutrition while elevating your salad to a level you once believed was unattainable!

Say goodbye to chemical-filled, oily dressings and hello to a new vibrant salad experience.

Mistake #6: The Wrong Mindset

Finally, the biggest mistake people commit is holding a negative or resistant mindset around salads. Instead of being excited to receive an abundance of nourishment from leafy greens, they see eating salad as an inconvenient chore that they begrudgingly must do.

Your mindset dictates your attitude, your attitude dictates your actions, and your actions dictate your results. Understand that the mindset with which you approach any goal will either support your efforts or sabotage them.

Be mindful of your internal dialogue and make an honest assessment of the mindset you are approaching your health goals with. It is essential to understand your core beliefs and why you believe them.

Many times we don't know why we believe something or how we came to believe it. However, if we simply ask the right questions, we can help ourselves uncover some of the unconscious programmed beliefs that no longer serve us.

On a piece of paper, write down and answer the following questions:

1. Do I want to be healthy? Why?

2. Do I deserve to have what I want? Why?

3. Do I have the power and ability to create the health and life I desire? How?

4. Do I believe eating leafy greens daily will benefit my health? How?

5. What are the top three reasons I am excited to eat more leafy greens?

6. What are three ways to accomplish my goal of eating more leafy greens each day?

7. How will I ensure that I succeed in accomplishing my health goals?

The first three questions will help you gain more awareness of the mindset and beliefs you hold about yourself and your life. If you are dissatisfied with these beliefs - just know that beliefs are merely thoughts that have been repeated enough times that they eventually became a belief. If you are intentional about improving the way you think and speak to yourself, you *will* change your beliefs and foster an attitude that empowers you to take action towards any goal.

The remaining four questions help you get clear on your beliefs about leafy greens. If you don't know why you want to eat more greens or if you even believe greens are healthy and necessary in your diet, then your attitude and actions will reflect that. Understanding your core beliefs around anything you are trying to do will allow you to take more conscious and effective action toward producing your desired results.

In the same way that repeated thoughts become core beliefs, repeated food choices become core cravings or desires. When you regularly eat leafy greens, even the pickiest eaters eventually enjoy them and even crave the taste and satisfaction of a big salad. So, work on developing a healthy mindset around leafy greens and get clear on your goals and beliefs. Once you do this, you will feel more confident, which will fuel a positive attitude, leading to constructive action and achieving your personal health goals.

Building Your Green-Esteem

A person's self-esteem is a measure of how they value and perceive themselves. We say someone with low self-esteem lacks confidence and has a negative opinion of who they are. Low self-esteem makes it difficult for a person to step outside their comfort zone or take any chances in the pursuit of accomplishing their goals.

Green-esteem, on the other hand, measures how a person values and perceives leafy greens. Someone with a low green-esteem turns their nose up at a salad and calls it tasteless rabbit food. They have diminished their ability to taste the depth of flavors in natural food and lack an appreciation for the immense value that greens have to offer. However, just as someone can improve their self-esteem, so too can they improve their green-esteem.

Building up your green-esteem will give you confidence in your ability to utilize and enjoy leafy greens in a variety of delicious ways, and deepen your respect for their health-promoting qualities. There are various ways to do this:

Green Smoothies

The key to raising your green-esteem is finding easy ways to sneak as many greens into your diet as possible. The more greens that find their way past your lips and into your gut to feed your microbiome, the faster your taste buds will begin to enjoy the taste.

Green smoothies are by far the easiest way for a beginner to get more greens into their diet. If you are hesitant to eat a big salad right away because you don't enjoy the taste of greens, starting out with a daily green smoothie is a great first step.

All you need to make a delicious green smoothie is:

1. **Fresh or frozen fruit**
   (Apples, bananas, mango, peaches, pineapple, pears, cherries, blueberries, strawberries, raspberries, blackberries, kiwi, papaya, persimmon, oranges, etc.)

2. **Leafy greens**
   (Spinach, collards, kale, arugula, romaine, bok choy, parsley, cilantro, basil, dill, cabbage, dandelion, lettuce, celery, spring mix, etc.)

3. **Clean water**
   (distilled, reverse osmosis, purified, etc.)

Initially, you will want to start out with much more fruit than greens in your smoothies. This will disguise the taste of the greens, but you still get all of their benefits! As your taste for greens evolves, you can increase the amount you add to the smoothies.

Everyone's preferences will be slightly different, but here are my basic green smoothie guidelines:

Green-Esteem Level	Fruits	Greens	Water
Low	80%	20%	1 to 3 cups
Average	50%	50%	1 to 3 cups
High	25%	75%	1 to 3 cups

If desired, you can also add one or two teaspoons of flax, chia, hemp, or walnuts to the smoothie for additional omega-3s.

I recommend using a high-speed blender (Vitamix, Blendtec, etc.) to give you the smoothest and creamiest green smoothies possible. There is nothing worse than a chunky green smoothie.

Pro Tip:
When making a smoothie, add the softest and juiciest ingredients to the blender first (closest to the blades) to help the blending process.

Even more ideal than a regular high-speed blender are vacuum blenders. These blenders remove most of the air from the container before blending to create less oxidation and nutrient loss. It may seem like a small detail, but you can truly taste the difference. Check out discountjuicers.com for great deals on vacuum blenders and other kitchen appliances.

Green Juices

Juicing is another fantastic way to get more leafy greens into your body and raise your green-esteem. While it is generally more time-consuming and more expensive than smoothies, many people still find it to be well worth the added effort.

Unlike green smoothies, which contain all of the fiber, green juices remove most of the fiber, providing a highly concentrated, nutrient-packed beverage. With green juice, you don't need to use as much sweet fruit to make it taste good. Instead, you can use vegetables like carrots or non-sweet fruits like cucumber to add a nice flavor to the juice.

For many people, juicing provides an appetizing way to increase their vegetable intake in parallel with consuming more greens. There are certainly ways to incorporate veggies, like carrots or fennel, into a smoothie, but it usually goes down much smoother in juice form.

To help you design your green juices, I've organized some commonly used ingredients below:

Mild Greens			
Butter lettuce	Green leaf lettuce	Red leaf lettuce	Romaine lettuce
Swiss chard	Spinach	Bok choy	Cilantro
Basil	Celery	Dill	Beet greens

Bitter Greens			
Kale	Collards	Arugula	Dandelion

Turnip greens	Mustard greens	Parsley	Radicchio
Radish greens	Celery leaves	Endive	Cabbage

Sweet Fruits			
Apples	Grapes	Pomegranate	Pears
Watermelon	Cantaloupe	Honeydew	Berries

Non-sweet Fruits			
Cucumber	Zucchini	Tomato	Peppers

Acid Fruits			
Orange	Lemon/Lime	Grapefruit	Pineapple

Sweet Vegetables			
Carrots	Sweet Potato	Jicama	Fennel

Earthy Vegetables			
Beets	Rutabaga	Turnip	Celeriac

Bitter Roots		Allium	
Ginger	Turmeric	Garlic	Onions/Shallots/Leeks

Again, everyone's preferences will be different, but to help you get started, I recommend the following green juice guidelines:

Green-Esteem Level	Greens	Primary Flavor Ingredient	Secondary Flavor Ingredient	Tertiary Flavor Ingredient
Low	Mild	Sweet fruits Acid fruits	Non-sweet fruits Sweet vegetables	Bitter Roots
Average	Mild or Bitter	Sweet fruits Sweet vegetables Earthy vegetables	Non-sweet fruits Acid fruits	Bitter Roots Allium
High	Bitter	Sweet vegetables Earthy vegetables	Non-sweet fruits Sweet fruits Acid fruits	Bitter Roots Allium

1. Use one or more ingredients from the categories listed in each column.
2. Tertiary flavor ingredients are optional.
3. Limit the total number of ingredients in each juice to 5 or less.
4. Start with sweeter juices until your green-esteem improves.

There are two main ways that you can make green juice:

Green Juice From a Juicer

The traditional way to make green juice is with a juicer. The best type of juicer to make green juice with is a masticating auger-style juicer that crushes the cell walls of the produce at a low rpm to extract the juice with minimal oxidation.

Pro Tip:
When adding your ingredients to the juicer, alternate back and forth between soft and firm ingredients for the best results.

I have used the Omega 8006 model juicer for over a decade and it has always produced great results. However, there are many newer juicers out there today that are worth considering.

Green Juice From a Blender

An alternative way to make green juice is with a blender and a nut milk bag. This method involves blending all of your ingredients in a blender with a little water and then straining it through a nut milk bag to remove the fiber. This is a great way to experiment with juicing without the need to buy a juicer.

While any blender would work, the best type of blender to make juice with is a vacuum blender. Removing most of the air before blending reduces oxidation of the juice and provides a more nutritious, flavorful, and smooth juice to enjoy.

If you already own a classic model of Vitamix blender, you might consider getting the BioChef Vacuum Blender Container + Pump. This vacuum container is compatible with the base of classic Vitamix models, but not the newer Ascent or Venturist models. This is a much less expensive way to make vacuum-blended juices and smoothies without needing to buy a whole new appliance.

Find Your Green Team

However you choose to raise your green-esteem, it is essential to do it in a supportive environment. I call this finding your Green Team, and it can be the difference between success and failure when it comes to reaching your health goals.

The way we eat is deeply intertwined with our social lives and being able to connect with others through the gift of food can be an important part of an overall healthy lifestyle. Unfortunately, many people attempt to get healthy in the company of health-resistant people, which makes reaching their goals even harder.

If you hang around people who love junk food and who ridicule your healthy choices, you are putting unnecessary and potentially insurmountable barriers between you and your goals. You must respect yourself enough to establish healthy boundaries with those you allow into your life if you want to maintain a healthy mindset and succeed with your goals.

Do your best to seek out and connect with others who are interested in healthy living and healthy food. You can do this through group coaching programs, membership groups, vegan Facebook groups, online communities, local meetups, and more!

Learning and growing together makes getting healthy a much more fun and enriching experience. Embark on healthy challenges, share recipes, and provide support and accountability to one another on your health journeys.

Do everything you can to surround yourself with a Green Team of salad lovers and truth seekers that will help you create an environment of health, positivity, and success!

7

The New Main Course

The time has come to translate everything we have discussed up to this point into something tangible that you can use to improve your life. It is one thing to know why we should eat more leafy greens, but it is another thing to have a clear vision and plan for implementing the information in a pragmatic way. In this chapter, we dive deeper into the details and action steps for creating a new main course that will revolutionize your meals.

This new main course is what I call a **5-Star Salad**. This is not your Grandma's salad. This salad has everything you could want from a main course, and nothing less. This is a salad with attitude and authority. 5-Star Salads combine volume, flavor, variety, and nutrition in a way that leaves you fully satisfied at the end of your meal.

Embracing 5-Star Salads as your new main course is more than just choosing a different meal - it's stepping into a new paradigm of self-empowerment and universal liberation.

It is time to acknowledge the sobering reality that food scientists pay their mortgage by getting you to repeatedly eat food-like products that make you sick. As you step into the 5-Star Salad paradigm, you have the opportunity to become your own food scientist and create meals with *real food* that hit all the bliss points, and give you all the satisfaction you desire - without chronic disease as a side effect! So grab your lab coat and a fork - class is in session.

The Science of Salads

The 5-Star Salad blueprint was scientifically formulated in the Raw Intuition Kitchen to light up your bliss points, activate your stretch receptors, and nourish every cell in your body. Through exhaustive human studies (on myself, friends, and family), I discovered there are three parameters that must be met in order to produce consistently positive results:

- **Structure**
- **Sense Appeal**
- **Satiation**

When my "study participants" were fed a salad that was formulated with these parameters in mind, I was able to consistently reproduce positive results. Not only did they feel great after their meal, but they reported experiencing fewer cravings and more control over their eating habits in the following days.

Their experiences corroborated my own, and at that point, I knew I had to recruit more participants. So now I invite you to take part in the *5-Star Salad Self-Report Study*, which I will explain in detail in the next chapter.

First, let's explore each variable more closely.

Structure

Creating structure in your life can reduce stress and boost your confidence and productivity. For example, having a morning routine, a workout plan, or a shopping list are all ways that someone can add structure and efficiency to their life.

In the same way that following a workout plan can help someone reach their fitness goals, I find a structured approach to making a salad provides a clear vision of what a healthy salad looks like, streamlines the process, and makes it easy to sustain a daily salad habit. Once you understand the framework of a 5-Star Salad, making delicious, satisfying salads becomes automatic.

There are five pillars that must be met to qualify as a 5-Star salad:

1. Include at least 1 pound (16 oz) of leafy greens
2. Include at least one type of cruciferous leafy green (kale, collars, arugula, cabbage, etc.)
3. Include at least one fresh herb (basil, cilantro, parsley, dill, etc.)
4. Include at least 5 different colors in your salad (red, orange, yellow, green, blue, purple, white, brown, etc.)
5. Include a flavorful, whole-food, plant-exclusive dressing

This is the framework that I have seen time and time again turn people with low green-esteem into avid salad lovers! I myself have been structuring my daily salads this way for about a decade, and I never tire of it!

For me, it wasn't just about making delicious salads to share with friends and family. I wanted to show them how easy it could be to make it for themselves. After all, if you give someone a 5-Star Salad, they eat well for a meal - but teach them to make their own, and they eat well for a lifetime.

The Pillars of a 5-Star Salad

The rating system works like this:

For each pillar that you incorporate into your salad, you receive one star. So, one pound of romaine lettuce with fresh dill, cucumber, tomatoes, and a store-bought ranch dressing would earn the following:

⭐ **One pound of romaine lettuce**

⭐ **Fresh dill**

That salad might have looked sufficient to an untrained eye, however, it was only worthy of a 2-Star rating.

If you took that same salad and added a cup of chopped arugula, some shredded carrots and beets, a half cup of sprouted lentils, and the Cajun Mango dressing from the *Recipe* section of this book, you would then earn:

⭐ **One pound of romaine lettuce**

⭐ **One cup of arugula (cruciferous green)**

⭐ **Fresh dill (herb)**

⭐ **Five different colors (green, red, purple, orange, yellow)**

⭐ **Flavorful, whole-food, plant-exclusive dressing**

With a few extra ingredients, we turned a mediocre 2-Star Salad into a mouth-watering 5-Star Salad worthy of being served as the main dish!

This shows how establishing the 5-star structure in your salad-building process can be the difference between a salad and a meal.

What Does One Pound of Greens Look Like?

The size and weight of a head or bunch of greens will vary, so it is useful to have a food scale in your kitchen to help you get accustomed to what this amount of greens looks like.

When making a 5-Star Salad, I will use around 12 oz of some type of lettuce as my base green. Then, I will add about 4 oz of cruciferous leafy greens as my "supplemental greens" to reach one pound (16 oz).

Below is a visual example of what this might look like:

Two-thirds (12 oz) of this large head of romaine lettuce   one (4 oz) head of baby bok choy.

Or

Two-thirds (12 oz) of this large head of romaine lettuce + 5 (4.76 oz) Brussels sprouts.

Or

Two-thirds (12 oz) of this large head of romaine lettuce + one heaping cup (4.22 oz) of finely chopped purple cabbage.

Or

Two-thirds (12 oz) of this large head of romaine lettuce + six leaves (4.07 oz) of dino kale.

The goal is not to be fixated on weighing your food but to have an accurate understanding of how much you're actually eating.

Many people think they eat more greens than they actually do, so testing their salads with a food scale can be an eye-opening experience.

Once you have a general understanding of what a pound of greens looks like, you won't need the scale anymore.

Sense Appeal

Every gratifying meal begins with our senses. From the moment we set our eyes on a potential meal, the body begins priming the digestive system. From the way our food looks, feels, smells, tastes, and sounds when we chew it - it all plays a role in the overall satisfaction that we experience from that meal.

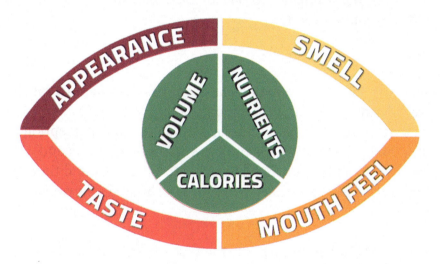

Appearance

It is said that we first eat with our eyes. Meaning the first thing that attracts us to a meal is how it looks. The visual appeal of food has always played a key role in human survival. Bright colors, like those in fruits and vegetables, signify energy and essential nutrients - like vitamin C. We are instinctually programmed to seek these colors in our food, which is why corporate marketing professionals use bright colors in product packaging.

When you are grocery shopping, do you select fruits and vegetables that look dull, shriveled, or bruised? Probably not, because in your conscious mind, you think that it will taste bad and you will waste your money. However, in your subconscious mind, your instincts recognize that it could make you sick or provide less energy - which in nature would make you vulnerable to predators.

This is why a 5-Star Salad is made with at least five different brightly colored fruits and vegetables. It not only looks delicious, but it appeals to our instinctual desire to consume brightly colored foods.

Smell

The smell of food is a major player in determining how much we will enjoy a meal. When food smells good to us, it increases our appetite and largely influences our perception of a food's flavor. This is why some amusement parks and restaurants diffuse artificial smells into the air around their business to increase their customer's desire and enjoyment of the food they serve.

However, Mother Nature was the first to use this tactic. Many fruits, for example, have a pleasantly strong fragrance when they are ripe and ready to be eaten. If you have ever picked fresh oranges from a tree or tomatoes from a garden, you know how incredible food is supposed to smell.

Unfortunately, most people have only eaten fruit from a grocery store, which is picked unripe and often lacks fragrance.

If you are like most people and you buy your fruits and vegetables from a grocery store, it is essential to tune into your senses to identify the highest quality produce that is available to you. When picking out the ingredients for your 5-Star Salad, the freshest and ripest ingredients will always make for the most enjoyable meal.

Feel

The feel of food matters. Not just how it feels in our hand but, more importantly, how it feels in our mouth. The food industry uses the term "mouth-feel" to describe the perfect amount of crunch or creaminess that keeps a person eating. The sensations that a food or drink creates in the mouth when consumed are key factors in how we perceive the dining experience.

You probably enjoy the sensation of biting into a nice, crisp apple versus a mealy one. Likewise, a mushy tomato or tough chunks of kale can ruin a person's salad experience. If you have ever taken a bit of salad and felt sand or dirt between your teeth, you know what a turn-off that can be. Once again, these are instinctual responses that our body uses to keep us from eating things that could make us sick or cause us harm.

This is another reason that choosing the highest quality ingredients and a few simple preparations can make all the difference in how much enjoyment you get from your 5-Star Salads. It only takes a moment to ensure you've rinsed the dirt off of the carrots and lettuce and finely chopped the tougher ingredients to create the most enjoyable mouth-feel from your meal.

Experiment with different cutting techniques to see which mouth feel you enjoy the most. Here are a few ways that I enjoy preparing my salads:

- Finely chop kale and tougher greens.

- Rough chop tender greens and lettuce - including boxed varieties.

- Shred or finely chop firm vegetables, like carrots and beets.

- Thinly slice onions, shallots, and leeks.

- Mix in heartier ingredients like sprouted lentils and peas for more texture.

- Use a creamy dressing from the *Recipe* section of this book rather than oil.

- Use a variety of soft, juicy, and crunchy ingredients to add contrast to the salad.

Taste

The most obvious aspect of a great salad is the taste. Just by addressing the previous three aspects, you will automatically improve the depth of flavor in your salads. However, the goal of a 5-Star Salad is to hit as many natural bliss points as possible, and you do that by being strategic with your ingredient selection.

Once again, a bliss point is the ideal amount of saltiness, sweetness, richness (fats), and also mouth feel in a food that stimulates the most dopamine or pleasure. While this concept is typically applied to processed foods, I find that it translates to healthy food as well.

If you can orchestrate the right amount of these flavor profiles together in your salads, you will generate more pleasure and satisfaction from the meal. This is the secret to retraining your brain and tastebuds to crave salad over chips and burgers. You will finally be able to eat the foods you enjoy while losing weight and lowering your risk of chronic disease.

Let's take a look at some examples of the ingredients that can be used to highlight each of the taste profiles in your salad:

Salty

Celery	Lemons	Limes	Tomatoes
Sun-dried tomatoes	Olives	Bok choy	Spinach
Chard	Dulce	Wakame	Nori
Oregano	Thyme	Hot peppers	Ginger

Sweet

Dates	Grapes	Raisins	Dried apricots
Mangoes	Figs	Cherries	Raspberries
Apples	Peas	Oranges	Papaya

Richness / Fattiness

Almonds	Avocado	Brazil nuts	Cashews
Chia seeds	Flax seeds	Hazelnuts	Hemp seeds
Macadamia nuts	Pecans	Pine nuts	Pistachios
Pumpkin seeds	Sesame seeds	Sunflower seeds	Walnuts
Nuts and seeds can be added whole, but I recommend blending them into a creamy salad dressing.			

Optimal Mouth Feel

Freshness	Crunchy	Chewy	Creamy
Firm vegetables	Apples	Raisins	Avocado
Crisp greens	Carrots	Dried apricots	Homemade Dressings
Crisp fruits	Celery	Dried cranberries	Mamey Sapote
Ripe fruits	Nuts / Seeds / Sprouts	Dried jackfruit	Cherimoya

Hitting Your Bliss Points

The fun part is that everyone has unique bliss points, based on their individual preferences. Some people like their meals saltier, while others like them sweeter. Your preferences might change depending on the day, but once you master the art of fine-tuning taste profiles and mouth feel, you can always create a meal that hits your bliss points.

To help you get started, I have provided some of my favorite blissful recipes at the end of this book.

Satiation

This is it! Are you ready? Perhaps the biggest reason 5-Star Salads are your greatest defense against cravings, bingeing, and dietary self-sabotage...

The third variable that makes 5-Star Salads such a powerful tool [on your wellness journey] is its ability to create superior satiation. It is not enough for a meal to look, smell, and taste good - it must also fill you with complete satisfaction. So, what is it that makes 5-Star Salads so gratifying? They go beyond tantalizing your outward-facing senses. A true 5-Star

Salad satisfies the deeper biological sensory pathways in your body that signal to your brain that you've been adequately nourished.

These pathways include stretch, nutrient, and calorie-sensing neurons located throughout the gastrointestinal tract that closely communicate with the brain to control appetite, satiation, and digestion.

Stretch Receptors

Containing at least one pound of leafy greens, in addition to all of the other fruits and vegetables, a 5-Star Salad is a high-volume meal. All that fiber and hydration fill the stomach and intestines, stretching their walls and activating mechanisms known as stretch receptors. These receptors signal to the brain that we have eaten enough food, which provokes hormonal changes that reduce or eliminate feelings of hunger.

Fiber and water are the superstars in this pathway, as they create the bulk that is needed to activate these receptors. Once activated, signals are sent through the vagus nerve to the brainstem and hypothalamus - the main areas of the brain that control appetite.

Nutrient Sensors

Throughout your gastrointestinal tract are sensory neurons that respond to the presence of nutrients. As nutrients are detected, hormones are released that notify the hypothalamus to begin down-regulating the hunger drive. There are more than twenty different gastrointestinal hormones involved in regulating appetite. These hormones induce sensory-specific satiety, which gradually reduces our desire to continue eating as the feeling of satiation sets in.

The high nutrient content of 5-Star Salads is the third superstar in this story. Between the leafy greens, the colorful fruits and vegetables, and the whole-food dressings, the nutrient profile of your salad is off the charts!

As you enjoy your delicious 5-Star salad, you saturate your gastrointestinal sensory neurons with a cornucopia of essential nutrients. These nutrients, combined with the bulk of water and fiber, create a powerful combination that satisfies the hunger drive from a cellular level.

Calorie Sensors

In addition to nutrient sensors, the brain and gastrointestinal tract also sense the caloric density of the foods we eat. It has been shown that neurons in the food-reward region of the brain, called the nucleus accumbens, are activated by calorie intake, independent of taste. As we discussed earlier, a higher caloric density increases the dopamine response mechanism that causes us to feel pleasure. Consequently, higher-calorie foods will stimulate more short-term pleasure than low-calorie foods.

Even though 5-Star Salads are comprised of relatively low-calorie ingredients, the synergy between the greens, fruits, vegetables, nuts, seeds, and spices creates a thoroughly pleasurable experience. This is a critical piece of the satiation equation because, without an adequate amount of pleasure stimulation from a meal, it will never fully satisfy us.

So, even though calories may not create satiation on their own, when they are consumed in the right context, such as a 5-Star Salad, they enhance the pleasure we get from eating healthy foods and contribute to our emotional satisfaction. This makes whole-food calories the fourth superstar in our 5-Star Salads.

Everyone's caloric needs are slightly different, but in general, I recommend that a 5-Star Salad contains roughly 500-700 calories (after the dressing is added) to ensure adequate pleasure and satiation.

Calorie counting, as a rule, is not something that I recommend. However, understanding the general calorie density of the ingredients you use in your salad can help you make adjustments if you feel you want more or fewer calories in your meal.

For example, according to cronometer.com, the salad listed below is 470 calories before the dressing is added.

After adding the dressing, the total calorie count was 769.

🍎 Lettuce, Romaine or Cos	1	head	106.42	kcal
🍎 Kale, Raw	2	cup, chopped	14.7	kcal
🍎 Tomato, Red, Raw	10	grape	14.22	kcal
🍎 Carrots, Raw	1	medium - 6" to 7" long	25.01	kcal
🍎 Mango, Fresh	1	cup	137.65	kcal
🍎 Raisins, Uncooked	0.25	cup, whole pieces	108.38	kcal
🍎 Onion, White, Yellow or Red, Raw	0.25	cup	19.41	kcal
🍎 Cilantro, Leaves, Raw	0.33	cup, chopped	1.21	kcal
🍎 Jalapeño Peppers, Raw	0.5	regular - approx 2" long	2.03	kcal
🍎 Lentil Sprouts, Raw	0.5	cup, whole pieces	40.81	kcal
🍎 Sunflower Seeds, Raw	3	tbsp, whole pieces	153.3	kcal
🍎 Dates, Medjool	2	date, pitted	132.96	kcal
🍎 Lemons, Raw	0.5	medium - 2 1/8" diameter	8.41	kcal
🍎 Mustard	0.5	tbsp	4.67	kcal

I find this to be a satisfying amount, but you will need to experiment and see what works best for you. It

The Satiation Superstar Team

To recap, the satiation superstars in your 5-Star Salad:

1. Fiber
2. Water
3. Nutrients
4. Whole-food calories

These are the key components that make your 5-Star Salad so satiating. None of these superstars can succeed without the others - it's a true team effort. However, the most important superstar that makes it all possible is YOU!

Without you taking proactive steps to actually eat more salad and take care of your health, none of the other superstars matter. So, whether or not you wear a cape at the dinner table, you are the real superstar!

Every Main Course Needs An Appetizer

I suggest starting your dinner with an appetizer of juicy fruit or a fruit-based smoothie roughly 20-30 minutes prior to eating your 5-Star Salad. This will add to your feeling of satiety at the end of the meal and reduce any chances of craving snacks after dinner.

I recommend that your appetizer be comprised of about 3-4 pieces of fresh fruit eaten whole or blended into a smoothie. This could be apples, pears, peaches, mangoes, oranges, a cantaloupe, or any other fresh fruit you enjoy.

> **Pro Tip:**
> **Enjoy your appetizer while you make your 5-Star Salad.**

Consciously Cooked Additions Are Optional

While the recipes provided in this book are raw, it is perfectly acceptable to use consciously cooked ingredients to supplement your 5-Star Salad. Conscious cooking refers to cooking methods that result in the least amount of damaging effects on the food - such as steaming, boiling, and pressure-cooking.

Cooking with dry heat, such as baking, grilling, or frying, creates harmful byproducts such as advanced glycation end products (AGEs), polycyclic aromatic hydrocarbons (PAHs), and acrylamide that can damage DNA and promote disease. Cooking with dry heat should be avoided as much as possible.

Some examples of consciously cooked additions that can be used in a 5-Star Salad include:

- Steamed potatoes (all varieties)
- Steamed squash
- Steamed mushrooms
- Vegetable soups and stews
- Pressure-cooked beans or lentils
- Pressure-cooked quinoa or wild rice

When adding consciously cooked ingredients to your 5-Star Salads, there is one guideline that I ask you to follow:

1. **Consciously cooked ingredients should <u>only</u> be added <u>after</u> you have eaten <u>at least half</u> of the raw salad.**

    When someone includes cooked food with their salad, oftentimes they end up eating so much of the cooked food that they can't finish their raw salad.

    By committing to eating at least half to three-quarters of your 5-Star Salad before any cooked food is consumed, you avoid the mistake of displacing the raw portion of your meal with cooked food.

Eating raw salad with consciously cooked food provides added enzymes, intact fiber, and hydration to encourage the proper digestion and elimination of the cooked food.

Designing Your Shopping List

Staple Items To Always Have On Hand

- **Leafy greens**: Rotate through as many different varieties as you can throughout each month. Have fun trying new types.

- **Vegetables**: Use as many different colors as you can. Each month, try including one new type of vegetable that you've never used before.

- **Medjool dates**: Dates are an essential staple ingredient for salad dressings.

- **Lemons**: Lemons get their own shout-out because they are a staple in salad dressings.

- **Fresh fruits**: Always have an ongoing rotation of seasonal, fresh fruits. You'll need a steady supply of fruit for your pre-dinner appetizers.

- **Frozen fruits**: Many frozen fruits (mango, blueberry, pineapple, etc.) can be used in salad dressings or added to a salad when fresh fruits are not available. If you live near a Costco, this is where I get the best deals on organic frozen fruits.

- **Dried herbs and spices**: Various dried herbs and spices are indispensable for making amazing salad dressings. Some of my favorites are basil, cayenne, cajun, chili flakes, chili powder, chipotle, chives, cinnamon, cumin, curry, dill, garlic granules, onion graduals, oregano, paprika (regular and smoked), pumpkin spice, rosemary, sage, taco, thyme, turmeric.

- **Nuts and seeds**: Nuts and seeds are the foundation of salad dressings. Some of my favorites are almonds, Brazil nuts, hemp seeds, macadamia nuts, pine nuts, sesame seeds, sunflower seeds, and pumpkin seeds.

Buying Your Greens

To make things as easy as possible, I recommend getting all of your greens in one trip at the beginning of the week or weekend.

You will need to buy at least (7) Base Greens, (4) Supplemental Greens, and (4) fresh herbs. Select any combination of greens from each category below to get the amounts needed.

The size of the head or bundle of greens will vary, so if your grocery store only has small heads, you may need to buy a few extra heads or bundles so that your salads are big enough each day.

You can buy boxed or bagged, pre-washed greens when needed, but I recommend buying as much of your greens as individual heads as you can if they are available.

To help you remember to rotate your greens, it can be helpful to buy whatever greens are on sale each week. Sales and discounted items are usually different each week, so pay attention to that. Rotating your greens will help you increase the diversity of plant species and different types of fibers in your diet.

Base Greens (x7)
- Iceberg lettuce
- Romaine lettuce
- Spinach
- Spring mix
- Butter lettuce
- Green leaf lettuce
- Red leaf lettuce

Supplemental Greens (x4)
- Arugula
- Beet greens
- Bok choy
- Cabbage
- Chard
- Collards
- Dandelion greens
- Endive
- Kale
- Mustard greens
- Radicchio

Fresh Herbs (x4)
- Basil
- Cilantro
- Dill
- Mint
- Parsley

Buying Your Vegetables

Vegetables are great at brightening up a salad and adding some incredible nutrition and sense appeal to the dish. Each week, you need to buy enough types of vegetables that will provide at least five different colors (in combination with the green from the leafy greens, and any colors from fruits in your salad) for that week's salads.

Each color represents a different phytonutrient (antioxidants, polyphenols, etc.) that will support a healthy gut microbiome.

Example:
Carrots (orange)
Onions (purple)
Tomatoes (red)
Summer squash (yellow)
Leafy greens (green)

The example above would satisfy the five different colors in your salad. Some other options you could choose from include:

Asparagus	Beets	Bell peppers	Broccoli
Carrots	Cauliflower	Celery	Corn
Cucumber	Fennel	Garlic	Ginger
Jalapeno	Leek	Mushrooms	Onions
Sprouts	Summer squash	Tomatoes	Zucchini

Buying Your Fruits

When it comes to buying fresh fruits, the variety will vary greatly, depending on the season. It is best to eat as locally-grown and in-season as possible but do not let the proximity of where the fruit is grown to deter you from enjoying a wide selection of delicious, nourishing varieties. Many fresh tropical fruits like mango, papaya, and pineapple can be found at lower prices from Asian Markets or wholesale suppliers.

The best deals on berries are most often going to be in the frozen section. Wholesale suppliers are usually the most economical option for buying berries.

Dates are used in the majority of my dressing recipes, so if you like my dressings, you will want to have a steady supply of dates on hand. I order eleven-pound cases from various date farms online - whichever one is offering the best deal at the time.

Each season has its own notable staple fruits that you can lean on throughout the year:

Spring Staple Fruits

Mango	Pineapple	Kiwi	Apricots
Bananas	Berries		

Summer Staple Fruits

Nectarines	Plums	Cherries	Peaches
Berries	Bananas	Mango	Melons
Papaya			

Autumn Staple Fruits

Apples	Figs	Grapes	Bananas
Papaya	Pomegranates	Persimmons	Pears

Winter Staple Fruits

Apples	Citrus	Dates	Bananas
Pears			

Time-Saving Tips

In case you are worried about the time commitment that it will take to make a 5-Star Salad every day, I wanted to provide a few tips to make the process more efficient for you.

1. **Buy all of the produce you need for the week on the same day/trip**
   There will of course be times when you'll need to make additional trips to the store, but if you can get the bulk of what you need in one trip, it will be much more convenient for you. This may require stops at multiple grocery stores to get everything you need, but it will save you time in the long run.

2. **Mass Prepare Your Ingredients**

   You can prepare enough salad ingredients for two or three salads at one time so all you have to do is throw everything together and enjoy!

   Using a food processor, it is easy to shred a bunch of carrots, beets, onions, jalapeños, bell peppers, or any other ingredients you want to include in your salads over the next few days. Keep everything in an air-tight glass container and use it all up within the next two days.

3. **Make Extra Dressing**

Salad dressings can last up to three days in the fridge - or up to a week if you use a vacuum blender and a sealed container. So make a few big batches of dressing and keep them in the fridge for faster dinner prep.

4. **Prepare Your Salads With Family or Friends**
If you eat dinner with a partner, family, or anyone else, make the salad prep a fun group activity. One person can chop the greens, and the other can make the dressing or prepare other ingredients. This makes cleanup a breeze as well.

5. Use The Right Tools For The Job

As I mentioned previously, one of the most effective ways to save time in the kitchen is to have the correct tools at your disposal. I've watched people try to prepare a salad with a steak knife and have a really tough time with it. So, ensure that you have a wide variety of knives, extra-large cutting boards, glass mason jars, extra-large salad bowls, a variety of glass storage containers, and whatever you feel that you will need to be successful.

Recommended Products and Tools

The tools we use can make all the difference in how we experience the 5-Star Salad lifestyle. The right kitchen tools make preparing meals easier, faster, and more enjoyable. You do not need to have the fanciest, most expensive tools available, but investing in high-quality tools and appliances for your kitchen is truly making an investment in your health.

Below are some of the tools that I recommend and where you can go to research them for yourself. As a disclaimer, these are my affiliate links. As an Amazon Associate, I earn a commission from purchases made with my links.

Blender

With a blender, you can turn a large amount of fruits and/or vegetables into tasty smoothies, dressings, soups, sauces, and more. The nice thing about blending is that it is quick, easy, and requires minimal cleanup.

Blending keeps the fiber in the end product, which is beneficial for digestion, helping us feel full as well as promoting healthy bowel movements.

What I use: Vitamix 5200 (You can purchase refurbished models at a discounted price at vitamix.com). I have used mine pretty much every day over the last ten years and it is still working great.

Check it out here: Vitamix Blender

What I recommend: Vacuum blending is what I now recommend to everyone I work with. I truly believe that vacuum blending is a revolutionary way to prepare smoothies, soups, sauces, and dips. By removing the air from the container before we blend, there is a substantial reduction in the oxidation of the food while blending - you can really see and taste the difference!

This equates to less nutrient loss, more antioxidants, more flavor, and smoother consistency. I use the BioChef Vacuum Blender Container + Pump which is compatible with my Vitamix base - which is an option for current Vitamix owners. If you do not already own a Vitamix, it is worth looking into vacuum blenders at http://discountjuicers.com/blenders.html.

Juicer

Juicing fruits and vegetables separates the liquid from the fiber. This gives you a highly concentrated source of nutrients that requires very little digestive energy.

Juicing requires more prep work and clean-up than blending, but many find the extra effort to be worth it.

A juicer is not required to succeed at raising your green-esteem, but I do enjoy juicing at times and believe that it is worth looking into if you are interested.

What I use: Omega 8006 - it has worked well for me over the last ten years and counting.

What I recommend: There are many newer juicers on the market today. I recommend researching the various brands at <u>Omega Juicer</u>.

Food Processor

A food processor is similar to a blender but is better for slicing, shredding, and chopping - it is not for making something into a smooth consistency. I like to use the food processor for making salsas, pico de gallo, pates, mock meats, guacamole, and shredding veggies.

What I use: Breville BFP660SIL Sous Chef 12 Cup Food Processor - This food processor makes recipe creations so easy - I love it.

What I recommend: This is the food processor that I recommend to anyone in the market for a food processor. You can look more into it at <u>Breville BFP660SIL Sous Chef 12 Cup Food Processor</u>.

Water Distiller

A water distiller purifies water by duplicating nature's hydrologic cycle of evaporation, condensation, and precipitation. As the water in the machine is heated, it turns to steam (leaving contaminants behind) and is then condensed and precipitates into your holding container as pure H2O.

Distillation is the most reliable method to purify water of all of the harmful contaminants that find their way into the water supply. This includes pesticides, pharmaceutical products, industrial waste, agricultural chemicals, inorganic minerals, and much more.

What I use: The [Pure Water Mini Classic CT Countertop Distiller](#) and the [AquaNui 8/5 Automatic Water Distiller](#) - I am an affiliate for both of these distillers.

What I recommend: If you are in the market for a water distiller, you can go to https://mypurewater.com or https://myaquanui.com and use my discount code (RAWINTUITION) for 5% off of your purchase.

If you are not looking to buy a water distiller, I recommend getting a few glass gallon jugs and filling them up at a reverse osmosis water dispenser at a local grocery store. Many grocery stores are now offering this service.

Cutting Boards

Cutting boards can be a hidden source of toxin exposure that you may have never considered. Plastic cutting boards can contaminate food with microplastics, phthalates, and Bisphenols. Many bamboo and wooded cutting boards are held together with wood glue and finish that has the potential to break down when exposed to alcohol, vinegar, or hot liquids.

What I use: 15.5" x 23" custom-made cutting board made from a single block of hard maple wood, free of petroleum-based finishes. We purchased it from treeboard.com. The specific board can be found here: https://treeboard.com/large-hard-maple-cutting-boards

What I recommend: Look for a nice glass or wooden cutting board that is around 14" x 17". Glass can be loud to cut on, which is why we ultimately ended up choosing a hard maple wood board that didn't use harsh glues or finishes.

Like anything else, it is an investment to equip your kitchen with quality, non-toxic products. If you are serious about upgrading your tools but can't do it all at once, just focus on one upgrade at a time, and over time you can make it happen.

Remember, don't let "perfect" be the enemy of good. Everything doesn't need to be perfect for you to take positive steps in the right direction. Establish what your priorities are and put your energy towards improving those areas. The important thing is to eat fruits and vegetables and to do the best you can.

Other Kitchen Essentials

These are my affiliate links. As an Amazon Associate, I earn a commission from purchases made with my links.

- Extra-large, salad bowls
- Glass "Ball" mason jars
- Citrus Juicer: Any brand
- Vacuum Lids for Mason Jars: SunnyPro Vacuum Lids 8.5cm

- <u>Chef knives and other-sized knives</u>: Any brand

- <u>Food Scale</u>: Etekcity Food Kitchen Scale

- <u>Glass Storage Containers</u>: Any brand

- <u>Vegetable peeler</u>: Any brand

- <u>Spiralizer</u>: Nuvantee Spiralizer

- <u>Julienne Peeler</u>: Kuhn Rikon, stainless steel

- Sprouting, Microgreens, and Gardening Seeds:

  <u>TrueLeafMarket.com</u>: High-Quality Sprout and Microgreens Seeds

  <u>sproutman.com</u>: High-Quality Sprouting Seeds

- <u>Salad spinner</u>: OXO Good Grips Large Salad Spinner

- <u>Liquid nutrients for indoor gardening</u>: OceanSolution 2-0-3

- <u>Shower Filter</u>: Aquasana.com

Follow The Salad Science

I hope I have shown you that when you build a salad with the right scientific formula: structure, sense appeal, and satiation factors - you cannot fail to create an incredibly delicious and satisfying meal.

You've learned about the health benefits of leafy greens, how to include them in your diet, how to grow them yourself, the myths about greens, how to find your green team, the importance of mindset, how to raise your green-esteem, and how to follow the salad science to improve your life.

Your next step is to put everything you've learned into practice. You have the information - now, it's up to you to take action.

8

Welcome To The Revolution

You are on the cusp of a **5-Star Salad Revolution**, where every fork-full of food brings you closer to the freedom you rightfully deserve. No more toxic hunger cravings, cheat days, or self-sabotage.

You have the blueprint for creating a new main course paradigm that will support your body, mind, and spirit in ways that you don't even realize yet. There is nothing more empowering and uplifting than fueling your body with the energy of raw, whole-plant foods.

It is time to declare your independence from the toxic-food industry and refuse to pollute your body and mind with food-like products that make you sick and unhappy. If it's made by man, think twice before putting it into your body. Become your own food scientist and create incredible food with the abundance of plants that Nature has to offer.

> **Genesis 1:29**
> *"And God said, Behold, I have given you every herb bearing seed, which is upon all the face of the earth, and every tree, in the which is the fruit of a tree yielding seed; to you it shall be for food."*

Join the *5-Star Salad Self-Report Study*

I invite you to take part in the **5-Star Salad Self-Report Study** to help me track the impact and results that people are experiencing from eating 5-Star Salads.

To be a part of the study, all you have to do is eat a 5-Star Salad (as described in this book) once a day for 14 days and answer a few simple questions.

Before you begin the 14-day period, write down your answer to the following questions:

1. On a scale of 1 (worst) - 10 (best), how much do you enjoy eating salads?

2. On average, how many days per week do you eat leafy greens?

3. On a scale of 1 (never) - 10 (every day), how often do you struggle with cravings for unhealthy foods?

4. On a scale of 1 (not at all) - 10 (constant struggle), how difficult is it for you to maintain your desired body weight?

5. On a scale of 1 (very poor) - 10 (flawless), how would you rate your digestive system function?

After you have eaten a 5-Star Salad, every day, for 14 days, please answer the following questions:

1. On a scale of 1 (worst) - 10 (best), how much do you enjoy eating salads?

2. On a scale of 1 (definitely not) - 10 (definitely yes), how likely are you to continue eating 5-Star Salads at least five times per week?

3. On a scale of 1 (not at all) - 10 (completely gone), how much have 5-Star Salads reduced your cravings for unhealthy foods?

4. On a scale of 1 (no difference) - 10 (great results), how have 5-Star Salads helped you achieve your desired body weight?

5. On a scale of 1 (no difference) - 10 (great results), how have 5-Star Salads helped your digestive system function?

6. Please share any additional feedback about your experience that you would like to.

Please email your answers to: Matt@Myrawintuition.com.

Your identity will never be shared, but data collected for this project may be shared in future projects or social media.

Thank you for your participation!

9

Recipes

Green Smoothies

If any ingredients are out of season or inaccessible, they can be swapped out with another similar fruit or leafy green.

Use these recipes as a guide to learning how to create your own combinations.

Blue Collard
2 cups collard greens, chopped (72 g / 2.5 oz)
3 medium navel oranges (400 g / 14 oz)
1 cup blueberries, fresh or frozen (148 g / 5 oz)
1 tsp maca powder (3 g / 0.1 oz)
1 tsp chia or flax seeds (3 g / 0.1 oz) (optional)
1 cup distilled water (237 g / 8 oz)

Add all ingredients to a blender.
Blend until smooth.

Kale Berry
2 cups kale, chopped (42 g / 1.5 oz)
4 mandarin oranges (352 g / 12 oz)
1 cup strawberries, fresh or frozen (152 g / 5.5 oz)
1 cup mango, fresh or frozen (229 g / 8 oz)
1 tsp chia or flax seeds (3 g / 0.1 oz) (optional)
1 cup distilled water (237 g / 8 oz)

Add all ingredients to a blender.
Blend until smooth.

Green Gulp
2 cups Spinach, chopped (60 g / 2 oz)
4 tangelos (380 g / 13.5 oz)
1 cup mango, fresh or frozen (229 g / 8 oz)
2 stalks celery (80 g / 3 oz)
1 tsp chia or flax seeds (3 g / 0.1 oz) (optional)
1 cup distilled water (237 g / 8 oz)

Add all ingredients to a blender.
Blend until smooth.

Bok On The Beach
2 cups bok choy, chopped (140 g / 5 oz)
2 bananas (236 g / 8 oz)
1 cup pineapple, fresh or frozen (165 g / 6 oz)
2 cups mango, fresh or frozen (458 g / 16 oz)
2 stalks celery (80 g / 3 oz)
1 tsp chia or flax seeds (3 g / 0.1 oz) (optional)
2 cups distilled water (474 g / 16 oz)

Add all ingredients to a blender.
Blend until smooth.

Kale Basil Blast
2 cups kale, chopped (42 g / 1.5 oz)
5 bananas (590 g / 21 oz)
1 cup blueberries, frozen (230 g / 8 oz)
1/4 cup basil, packed (10.5 g / .5 oz)
1 tsp chia or flax seeds (3 g / 0.1 oz) (optional)
2 cups distilled water (474 g / 16 oz)

Add all ingredients to a blender.
Blend until smooth.

Chocolate Shake
2 cups romaine lettuce, chopped (94 g / 3.5 oz)
5 bananas (590 g / 21 oz)
4 medjool dates (96 g / 3.5 oz)
1 Tbsp carob or cacao powder (6 g / .2 oz)
1 cup distilled water (237 g / 8 oz)

Add all ingredients to a blender.
Blend until smooth.

Romaine Empire
2 cups romaine lettuce, chopped (94 g / 3.5 oz)
5 bananas (590 g / 21 oz)
2 mandarin oranges (176 g / 6 oz)
1 cup frozen cherries (140 g / 5 oz)
2 stalks celery (80 g / 3 oz)
1/3 cup cilantro, packed (5 g / .2 oz)
1 tsp chia or flax seeds (3 g / 0.1 oz) (optional)
2 cups distilled water (474 g / 16 oz)

Add all ingredients to a blender.
Blend until smooth.

Pear Zinger
2 cups arugula, chopped (40 g / 1.5 oz)
2 Bartlett pears (354 g / 12.5 oz)
1 cup pineapple, fresh or frozen (165 g / 6 oz)
2 stalks celery (80 g / 3 oz)
2 Medjool dates, pitted (48 g / 1.5 oz)
2 cups distilled water (474 g / 16 oz)

Add all ingredients to a blender.
Blend until smooth.

Pear-A-Dice
2 cups butter lettuce (85 g / 3 oz)
2 Bartlett pears (354 g / 12.5 oz)
2 Navel oranges (262 g / 9 oz)
2 stalks celery (80 g / 3 oz)
2 Medjool dates, pitted (48 g / 1.5 oz)
1 tsp chia or flax seeds (3 g / 0.1 oz) (optional)
1 cup distilled water (237 g / 8 oz)

Add all ingredients to a blender.
Blend until smooth.

Berry Mango Glory
2 cups spinach (60 g / 2 oz)
1/4 cup basil, packed (10.5 g / .5 oz)
5 bananas (590 g / 21 oz)
1 cup frozen berry mix (126 g / 4/5 oz)
1 cup mango, fresh or frozen (229 g / 8 oz)
1 tsp maca powder (5 g / .2 oz)
2 cups distilled water (474 g / 16 oz)

Add all ingredients to a blender.
Blend until smooth.

Green Juices

True Green
5 cups spinach (150 g / 5 oz)
5 stalks celery (200 g / 7 oz)
2 granny smith apples (334 g / 11.5 oz)
1 lemon (58 g / 2 oz)
1 cucumber (216 g / 7.5 oz)

Juice and enjoy.

Ginger Romaine
5 cups romaine lettuce (235 g / 8 oz)
1 bunch parsley (60 g / 2 oz)
5 carrots (305 g / 10.5 oz)
2 navel oranges (262 g / 9 oz)
1 thumb of ginger (25 g / 1 oz)

Juice and enjoy.

Purple Potion
3 cups bok choy (210 g / 7.5 oz)
2 cups purple cabbage (178 g / 6 oz)
1/2 beet (45 g / 2 oz)
1 lemon (58 g / 2 oz)
2 sweet apples (364 g / 13 oz)
5 carrots (305 g / 10.5 oz)

Juice and enjoy.

Liver Massage
5 cups kale (105 g / 3.5 oz)
3 navel oranges (393 g / 14 oz)
1/2 lemon (29 g / 1 oz)
1 bunch cilantro (16 g / .5 oz)
1 cup dandelion greens (55 g / 2 oz)
1 pinky of turmeric (15 g / .5 oz)

Juice and enjoy.

Pineapple Mint Tonic
3 cups arugula (60 g / 2 oz)
2 cups spinach (60 g / 2 oz)
2 cups pineapple (330 g / 12 oz)
2 sweet apples (364 g / 13 oz)
2 sprigs of mint (6 g / .2 oz)

Juice and enjoy.

Fennel Therapy
5 cups romaine lettuce (235 g / 8 oz)
1 cucumber (216 g / 7.5 oz)
2 sweet apples (364 g / 13 oz)
1 lemon (58 g / 2 oz)
1 bulb of fennel (234 g / 8 oz)
6 stalks celery (240 g / 8.5 oz)

Juice and enjoy.

I'll Be Bok
3 cups collard greens (108 g / 4 oz)
2 cups bok choy (140 g / 5 oz)
2 sweet apples (364 g / 13 oz)
1/2 red bell pepper (60 g / 2 oz)
1 lemon (58 g / 2 oz)
1 thumb ginger (25 g / 1 oz)

Juice and enjoy.

Dill And Chill
5 cups spinach (150 g / 5 oz)
1 cucumber (216 g / 7.5 oz)
5 stalks celery (200 g / 7 oz)
2 sweet apples (364 g / 13 oz)
1 lemon (58 g / 2 oz)
1 bunch dill (9 g / .3 oz)

Juice and enjoy.

Green Earth
5 cups kale (105 g / 3.5 oz)
1 bunch parsley (60 g / 2 oz)
7 carrots (427 g / 15 oz)
1 beet (90 g / 4 oz)
1 thumb ginger (25 g / 1 oz)
1 lemon (58 g / 2 oz)

Juice and enjoy.

Tangelo Twister
5 cups romaine lettuce (235 g / 8 oz)
1 bunch cilantro (16 g / .5 oz)
5 carrots (305 g / 10.5 oz)
3 tangelo oranges (393 g / 14 oz)

Juice and enjoy.

Salad Dressings

The following salad dressings are designed to hit your bliss points so that your 5-Star Salad is exceptionally enjoyable.

Each salad dressing recipe can be used all at once as a single serving or split into two servings, depending on how much dressing you prefer.

Macarena (Makes 1 - 2 Servings)
2 Tbsp macadamia nuts (16 g / .5 oz)
1 Tbsp hemp seeds (10 g / .3 oz)
1/2 lemon, peeled (29 g / 1 oz)
1 mandarin orange (88g / 3 oz)
2 Medjool dates, pitted (48 g / 1.5 oz)
1 clove garlic (3 g / .1 oz)
2 tsp maca powder (10 g / .3 oz)
3/4 cup distilled water (178 g / 6 oz)

Add all ingredients to a blender.
Blend until smooth.

Onion and Chive (Makes 1 - 2 Servings)
2 Tbsp hemp seeds (20 g / .6 oz)
1 Tbsp macadamia nuts (8 g / .3 oz)
2 Medjool dates, pitted (48 g / 1.5 oz)
1/2 lemon, peeled (29 g / 1 oz)
1 clove garlic (3 g / .1 oz)
2 tsp chives, dried (.2 g)
1 tsp onion granules (2 g)
1 tsp brown mustard (5 g)
3/4 cup distilled water (178 g / 6 oz)

Add all ingredients to a blender.
Blend until smooth.

Creamy Oregano (Makes 1 - 2 Servings)
3 Tbsp sesame seeds (27 g / 1 oz)
2 Medjool dates, pitted (48 g / 1.5 oz)
1/2 lemon, peeled (29 g / 1 oz)
1 clove garlic (3 g / .1 oz)
1 tsp oregano, dried (1 g)
3/4 cup distilled water (178 g / 6 oz)

Add all ingredients to a blender.
Blend until smooth.

Smokey Chive (Makes 1 - 2 Servings)
2 Tbsp Brazil nuts (20 g / .7 oz)
1 Tbsp hemp seeds (10 g / .3 oz)
2 Medjool dates, pitted (48 g / 1.5 oz)
1/2 lemon, peeled (29 g / 1 oz)
3 tsp nutritional yeast (4 g / .1 oz)
1 tsp onion granules (2 g)
1 tsp chives, dried (.1 g)
1/2 tsp smoked paprika (1 g)
1/8 tsp cayenne pepper
3/4 cup distilled water (178 g / 6 oz)

Add all ingredients to a blender.
Blend until smooth.

Cranberry Anise (Makes 1 - 2 Servings)
2 Tbsp hemp seeds (20 g / .6 oz)
1 Tbsp sesame seeds (9 g / .3 oz)
2 Medjool dates, pitted (48 g / 1.5 oz)
1/2 lemon, peeled (29 g / 1 oz)
1 clove garlic (3 g / .1 oz)
1/4 cup cranberries, dried (40 g / 1.5 oz)
1 tsp anise seeds (2 g)
3/4 cup distilled water (178 g / 6 oz)

Add all ingredients to a blender.
Blend until smooth.

Purple Haze (Makes 1 - 2 Servings)
3 Tbsp sesame seeds (27 g / 1 oz)
2 Medjool dates, pitted (48 g / 1.5 oz)
1/2 lemon, peeled (29 g / 1 oz)
1 tsp onion granules (2 g)
1 tsp sage, dried (.3 g)
2 tsp dulce flakes
1/8 tsp cayenne pepper
3/4 cup distilled water (178 g / 6 oz)

Add all ingredients to a blender.
Blend until smooth.

Pickle Spice (Makes 1 - 2 Servings)
3 Tbsp sunflower seeds (27 g / 1 oz)
2 Medjool dates, pitted (48 g / 1.5 oz)
1/2 lemon, peeled (29 g / 1 oz)
1 clove garlic (3 g / .1 oz)
1 tsp pickle spice seasoning (4 g / .1 oz)
3/4 cup distilled water (178 g / 6 oz)

Add all ingredients to a blender.
Blend until smooth.

Macadamia Fire (Makes 1 - 2 Servings)
3 Tbsp Macadamia nuts (27 g / 1 oz)
2 Medjool dates, pitted (48 g / 1.5 oz)
1/2 lemon, peeled (29 g / 1 oz)
1/2 tsp onion granules (1 g)
1 tsp paprika (2 g)
1/3 tsp chipotle powder
1/2 jalapeño (with seeds) (15 g / .5 oz)
3/4 cup distilled water (178 g / 6 oz)

Add all ingredients to a blender.
Blend until smooth.

Macadill Ranch (Makes 1 - 2 Servings)
3 Tbsp macadamia nuts (27 g / 1 oz)
2 Medjool dates, pitted (48 g / 1.5 oz)
1/2 lemon, peeled (29 g / 1 oz)
1 clove garlic (3 g / .1 oz)
1 tsp dill, dried (1 g)
1 tsp chives, dried (.1 g)
3/4 cup distilled water (178 g / 6 oz)

Add all ingredients to a blender.
Blend until smooth.

Cuminator (Makes 1 - 2 Servings)
3 Tbsp sunflower seeds (27 g / 1 oz)
2 Medjool dates, pitted (48 g / 1.5 oz)
1/2 lemon, peeled (29 g / 1 oz)
1/2 tsp cumin (1 g)
1 tsp onion granules (2 g)
1/2 tsp red pepper flakes (1 g)
1/4 cup red bell pepper, fresh (40 g / 1.5 oz)
3/4 cup distilled water (178 g / 6 oz)

Add all ingredients to a blender.
Blend until smooth.

Fentastic (Makes 1 - 2 Servings)
3 Tbsp pumpkin seeds (23 g / .8 oz)
2 Medjool dates, pitted (48 g / 1.5 oz)
1/2 lemon, peeled (29 g / 1 oz)
1 medium navel orange, peeled (131 g / 4.5 oz)
1 clove garlic (3 g / .1 oz)
1 tsp fennel seed powder (2 g)
3/4 cup distilled water (178 g / 6 oz)

Add all ingredients to a blender.
Blend until smooth.

Brazilian Heat (Makes 1 - 2 Servings)
2 Tbsp Brazil nuts (20 g / .7 oz)
1 Tbsp hemp seeds (10 g / .3 oz)
2 Medjool dates, pitted (48 g / 1.5 oz)
1/2 lemon, peeled (29 g / 1 oz)
1 clove garlic (3 g / .1 oz)
1 pinky of ginger, fresh (15 g / .5 oz)
1 tsp red pepper flakes (2 g)
1 tsp paprika (2 g)
1 tsp yellow mustard (4 g)
3/4 cup distilled water (178 g / 6 oz)

Add all ingredients to a blender.
Blend until smooth.

Cajun Mango (Makes 1 - 2 Servings)
3 Tbsp Brazil nuts (30 g / 1 oz)
2 Medjool dates, pitted (48 g / 1.5 oz)
1/2 lemon, peeled (29 g / 1 oz)
1 cup mango, fresh or thawed (229 g / 8 oz)
1 clove garlic (3 g / .1 oz)
1 tsp cajun seasoning (.6 g)
3/4 cup distilled water (178 g / 6 oz)

Add all ingredients to a blender.
Blend until smooth.

Mango Thyme (Makes 1 - 2 Servings)
3 Tbsp hemp seeds (30 g / 1 oz)
2 Medjool dates, pitted (48 g / 1.5 oz)
1/2 lemon, peeled (29 g / 1 oz)
1 cup mango, fresh or thawed
1/2 tsp onion granules (1 g)
1 tsp thyme, dried (3 g)
3/4 cup distilled water (178 g / 6 oz)

Add all ingredients to a blender.
Blend until smooth.

Mango Red (Makes 1 - 2 Servings)
3 Tbsp hemp seeds (30 g / 1 oz)
2 Medjool dates, pitted (48 g / 1.5 oz)
1/2 lemon, peeled (29 g / 1 oz)
1 cup mango, fresh or thawed (229 g / 8 oz)
1/3 cup red bell pepper, fresh (30 g / 1 oz)
1 clove garlic (3 g / .1 oz)
1/2 tsp smoked paprika (1 g)
1/2 tsp red pepper flakes (1 g)
1/2 tsp cilantro, dried (.3 g)
3/4 cup distilled water (178 g / 6 oz)

Add all ingredients to a blender.
Blend until smooth.

Southwest Chipotle (Makes 1 - 2 Servings)
3 Tbsp sunflower seeds (27 g / 1 oz)
2 Medjool dates, pitted (48 g / 1.5 oz)
1/2 lemon, peeled (29 g / 1 oz)
1 tsp onion granules (2 g)
3/4 tsp chipotle powder (1 g)
2 tsp brown mustard (8 g / .3 oz)
3/4 cup distilled water (178 g / 6 oz)

Add all ingredients to a blender.
Blend until smooth.

Sesame Nori (Makes 1 - 2 Servings)
2 Tbsp sesame seeds (18 g / .6 oz)
1 Tbsp hemp seeds (10 g / .4 oz)
2 Medjool dates, pitted (48 g / 1.5 oz)
1/2 lemon, peeled (29 g / 1 oz)
1 sheet of nori (seaweed) (2 g)
1 clove garlic (3 g / .1 oz)
1 tsp dill, dried (1 g)
1 tsp sage, dried (.3 g)
1 cup distilled water (178 g / 6 oz)

Add all ingredients to a blender.
Blend until smooth.

Fat-Free Salad Dressings

Frawnch (Makes 1 Serving)
1.5 cups vine tomatoes, chopped (270 g / 9.5 oz)
1 clove garlic (3 g / .1 oz)
1 tsp onion granules (2 g)
4 medjool dates (96 g / 3 oz)
1/2 lemon, peeled (29 g / 1 oz)

Add all ingredients to a blender.
Blend until smooth.

Honey-Less Mustard (Makes 1 Serving)
5 Medjool dates (120 g / 4.25 oz)
2 Tbsp dijon mustard (30 g / 1 oz)
1 tsp garlic granules (2 g)
Pinch of black pepper
3/4 cup distilled water (178 g / 6 oz)

Add all ingredients to a blender.
Blend until smooth.

Apricot Infusion (Makes 1 Serving)
8 apricots, dried (65 g / 2.3 oz)
1 lemon, peeled (58 g / 2 oz)
1 tsp chili powder (2 g)
1 tsp onion granules (2 g)
1 cup distilled water (226 g / 8 oz)

Add all ingredients to a blender.
Blend until smooth.

Purple Surge (Makes 1 Serving)
1/2 cup raisins (73 g / 2.5 oz)
1/3 cup red bell pepper, chopped (50 g / 1.75 oz)
1 lemon, peeled (58 g / 2 oz)
1/2 cup distilled water (113 g / 4 oz)

Add all ingredients to a blender.
Blend until smooth.

Black Magic (Makes 1 Serving)
6 black mission figs, dried (68 g / 2.4 oz)
2 tsp dijon mustard (10 g / .35 oz)
1/2 lemon, peeled (29 g / 1 oz)
1 tsp onion granules (2 g)
1 tsp garlic granules (2 g)
1 cup distilled water (226 g / 8 oz)

Add all ingredients to a blender.
Blend until smooth.

5-Star Salads

If any of the ingredients are out of season or inaccessible, they can be swapped out with another similar ingredient.

The goal is to be able to create a 5-Star Salad with whatever fresh produce you have in your fridge, without having to think about specific recipes.

So, use these recipes as a guide to learning how to create your own variations of a 5-Star Salad.

The Pillars of a 5-Star Salad

Cajun Berry Mango 5-Star Salad
1 large head of red leaf lettuce, chopped (360 g / 12 .5 oz)
4 medium leaves of kale, finely chopped (112 g / 4 oz)
1/4 cup cilantro, chopped (4 g / .1 oz)
2 carrots, shredded or chopped (120 g / 4 oz)
1/4 cup red onion, chopped (50 g / 1.75 oz)
1/2 jalapeño, sliced (7 g / .25 oz)
1/2 cup strawberries, halved (75 g / 2.5 oz)
1 cup mango, fresh or thawed (229 g / 8 oz)
7 - 10 grape tomatoes, halved (70 g / 2.5 oz)

Add all of the ingredients to a large salad bowl and mix well.

Dressing: Cajun Mango (Makes 1 - 2 Servings)
3 Tbsp Brazil nuts (30 g / 1 oz)
2 Medjool dates, pitted (48 g / 1.5 oz)
1/2 lemon, peeled (29 g / 1 oz)
1 cup mango, fresh or thawed (229 g / 8 oz)
1 clove garlic (3 g / .1 oz)
1 tsp cajun seasoning (.6 g)
3/4 cup distilled water (178 g / 6 oz)

Add all ingredients to a blender.
Blend until smooth.

Citrus Herb 5-Star Salad
1 large head of green leaf lettuce, chopped (360 g / 12 .5 oz)
5 cups arugula, chopped (100 g / 3.5 oz)
1/4 cup basil, chopped (10 g / .35 oz)
1/4 cup red onion, chopped (50 g / 1.75 oz)
1/2 medium cucumber, sliced (112 g / 4 oz)
2 mandarin oranges (176 g / 6 oz)
1/2 cup dried apricots, chopped (70 g / 2.5 oz)
7 - 10 grape tomatoes, halved (70 g / 2.5 oz)

Add all of the ingredients to a large salad bowl and mix well.

Dressing: Onion and Chive (1 - 2 Servings)
2 Tbsp hemp seeds (20 g / .6 oz)
1 Tbsp macadamia nuts (8 g / .3 oz)
2 Medjool dates, pitted (48 g / 1.5 oz)
1/2 lemon, peeled (29 g / 1 oz)
1 clove garlic (3 g / .1 oz)
2 tsp chives, dried (.2 g)
1 tsp onion granules (2 g)
1 tsp brown mustard (5 g)
3/4 cup distilled water (178 g / 6 oz)

Add all ingredients to a blender.
Blend until smooth.

Apple Berry 5-Star Salad
1 large head of romaine lettuce, chopped (360 g / 12 .5 oz)
5 cups arugula, chopped (100 g / 3.5 oz)
1/4 cup cilantro, chopped (4 g / .1 oz)
1/4 cup sweet onion, chopped (50 g / 1.75 oz)
1/3 cup red bell pepper, chopped (50 g / 1.75 oz)
1 sweet apple, chopped or sliced (175 g / 6 oz)
1/2 cup blueberries, fresh or thawed (75 g / 2.6 oz)
7 - 10 grape tomatoes, halved (70 g / 2.5 oz)

Add all ingredients to a large salad bowl and mix well.

Dressing: Cranberry Anise (Makes 1 - 2 Servings)
2 Tbsp hemp seeds (20 g / .6 oz)
1 Tbsp sesame seeds (9 g / .3 oz)
2 Medjool dates, pitted (48 g / 1.5 oz)
1/2 lemon, peeled (29 g / 1 oz)
1 clove garlic (3 g / .1 oz)
1/4 cup cranberries, dried (40 g / 1.5 oz)
1 tsp anise seeds (2 g)
3/4 cup distilled water (178 g / 6 oz)

Add all ingredients to a blender.
Blend until smooth.

Cumin Get It 5-Star Salad
1 large head of green leaf lettuce, chopped (360 g / 12 .5 oz)
1.5 cups purple cabbage, finely chopped (133 g / 4.7 oz)
1/4 cup parsley, chopped (15 g / .5 oz)
2 carrots, shredded or chopped (120 g / 4 oz)
1/2 cup mushrooms, chopped or sliced (48 g / 1.7 oz)
1/2 cup organic corn, fresh or thawed (72 g / 2.5 oz)
1/4 cup red onion, chopped (50 g / 1.75 oz)
1/2 jalapeño, sliced (7 g / .25 oz)
7 - 10 grape tomatoes, halved (70 g / 2.5 oz)

Add all ingredients to a large salad bowl and mix well.

Dressing: Cuminator (1 - 2 Servings)
3 Tbsp sunflower seeds (27 g / 1 oz)
2 Medjool dates, pitted (48 g / 1.5 oz)
1/2 lemon, peeled (29 g / 1 oz)
1/2 tsp cumin (1 g)
1 tsp onion granules (2 g)
1/2 tsp red pepper flakes (1 g)
1/4 cup red bell pepper, fresh (40 g / 1.5 oz)
3/4 cup distilled water (178 g / 6 oz)

Add all ingredients to a blender.
Blend until smooth.

Pineapple Raspberry 5-Star Salad
1 large head of red leaf lettuce, chopped (360 g / 12 .5 oz)
4 medium leaves of kale, finely chopped (112 g / 4 oz)
1/4 cup basil, chopped (10 g / .35 oz)
1/4 cup yellow onion, chopped (50 g / 1.75 oz)
1/3 cup beet, shredded (95 g / 3.35 oz)
1/2 cup raspberries, fresh or thawed (60 g / 2.1 oz)
1 cup pineapple, fresh or thawed (165 g / 5.8 oz)
7 - 10 grape tomatoes, halved (70 g / 2.5 oz)

Add all ingredients to a large salad bowl and mix well.

Dressing: Creamy Oregano (1 - 2 Servings)
3 Tbsp sesame seeds (27 g / 1 oz)
2 Medjool dates, pitted (48 g / 1.5 oz)
1/2 lemon, peeled (29 g / 1 oz)
1 clove garlic (3 g / .1 oz)
1 tsp oregano, dried (1 g)
3/4 cup distilled water (178 g / 6 oz)

Add all ingredients to a blender.
Blend until smooth.

Basil Mango Thyme 5-Star Salad
1 large head of red leaf lettuce, chopped (360 g / 12 .5 oz)
1.5 cups bok choy, chopped (105 g / 3.7 oz)
1/4 cup basil, chopped (10 g / .35 oz)
1/4 cup red onion, chopped (50 g / 1.75 oz)
2 stalks celery, chopped (80 g / 2.8 oz)
1/2 cup green peas, fresh or thawed (80 g / 2.8 oz)
1 cup red grapes, halved (151 g / 5.3 oz)
7 - 10 grape tomatoes, halved (70 g / 2.5 oz)

Add all ingredients to a large salad bowl and mix well.

Dressing: Mango Thyme (1 - 2 Servings)
3 Tbsp hemp seeds (30 g / 1 oz)
2 Medjool dates, pitted (48 g / 1.5 oz)
1/2 lemon, peeled (29 g / 1 oz)
1 cup mango, fresh or thawed
1/2 tsp onion granules (1 g)
1 tsp thyme, dried (3 g)
3/4 cup distilled water (178 g / 6 oz)

Add all ingredients to a blender.
Blend until smooth.

Pineapple Ranch 5-Star Salad
1/2 large head iceberg lettuce, chopped (375 g / 13 oz)
4 medium leaves of kale, finely chopped (112 g / 4 oz)
1/4 cup dill, chopped (3 g / .1 oz)
1/4 cup red onion, chopped (50 g / 1.75 oz)
1/2 cucumber, sliced (112 g / 4 oz)
1/3 cup beet, shredded (95 g / 3.35 oz)
1 cup pineapple, fresh or thawed (165 g / 5.8 oz)
7 - 10 grape tomatoes, halved (70 g / 2.5 oz)

Add all ingredients to a large salad bowl and mix well.

Dressing: Macadill Ranch (1 - 2 Servings)
3 Tbsp macadamia nuts (27 g / 1 oz)
2 Medjool dates, pitted (48 g / 1.5 oz)
1/2 lemon, peeled (29 g / 1 oz)
1 clove garlic (3 g / .1 oz)
1 tsp dill, dried (1 g)
1 tsp chives, dried (.1 g)
3/4 cup distilled water (178 g / 6 oz)

Add all ingredients to a blender.
Blend until smooth.

Cranberry Macarena 5-Star Salad
1 large head of red leaf lettuce, chopped (360 g / 12 .5 oz)
4 medium leaves of kale, finely chopped (112 g / 4 oz)
1/4 cup cilantro, chopped (4 g / .1 oz)
1/4 cup yellow onion, chopped (50 g / 1.75 oz)
2 carrots, shredded or chopped (120 g / 4 oz)
1/2 cucumber, sliced (112 g / 4 oz)
1/4 cup dried cranberries (40 g / 1.4 oz)
1/3 cup raisins (50 g / 1.75 oz)
7 - 10 grape tomatoes, halved (70 g / 2.5 oz)

Add all ingredients to a large salad bowl and mix well.

Dressing: Macarena (1 - 2 Servings)
2 Tbsp macadamia nuts (16 g / .5 oz)
1 Tbsp hemp seeds (10 g / .3 oz)
1/2 lemon, peeled (29 g / 1 oz)
1 mandarin orange (88g / 3 oz)
2 Medjool dates, pitted (48 g / 1.5 oz)
1 clove garlic (3 g / .1 oz)
2 tsp maca powder (10 g / .3 oz)
3/4 cup distilled water (178 g / 6 oz)

Add all ingredients to a blender.
Blend until smooth.

Spicy Mango Red 5-Star Salad
2 heads of butter lettuce, chopped (340 g / 12 oz)
1.5 cups red cabbage, finely chopped (133 g / 4.7 oz)
1/4 cup parsley, chopped (15 g / .5 oz)
1/4 cup shallots, chopped (40 g / 1.4 oz)
2 carrots, shredded or chopped (120 g / 4 oz)
1/2 jalapeño, sliced (7 g / .25 oz)
1/2 cup red grapes, halved (75 g / 2.6 oz)
1/2 cucumber, sliced (112 g / 4 oz)
7 - 10 grape tomatoes, halved (70 g / 2.5 oz)

Add all ingredients to a large salad bowl and mix well.

Dressing: Mango Red (1 - 2 Servings)
3 Tbsp hemp seeds (30 g / 1 oz)
2 Medjool dates, pitted (48 g / 1.5 oz)
1/2 lemon, peeled (29 g / 1 oz)
1 cup mango, fresh or thawed (229 g / 8 oz)
1/3 cup red bell pepper, fresh (30 g / 1 oz)
1 clove garlic (3 g / .1 oz)
1/2 tsp smoked paprika (1 g)
1/2 tsp red pepper flakes (1 g)
1/2 tsp cilantro, dried (.3 g)
3/4 cup distilled water (178 g / 6 oz)

Add all ingredients to a blender.
Blend until smooth.

Macadamia Fire 5-Star Salad
1 large head of romaine lettuce, chopped (360 g / 12 .5 oz)
4 medium leaves of kale, finely chopped (112 g / 4 oz)
1/4 cup parsley, chopped (15 g / .5 oz)
2 green onions, finely sliced (24 g / .85 oz)
2 carrots, shredded or chopped (120 g / 4 oz)
1 cup navel oranges, chopped (165 g / 5.8 oz)
1 cup mango, fresh or thawed (229 g / 8 oz)
1/3 cup red bell pepper, chopped (30 g / 1 oz)
7 - 10 grape tomatoes, halved (70 g / 2.5 oz)

Add all ingredients to a large salad bowl and mix well.

Dressing: Macadamia Fire (1 - 2 Servings)
3 Tbsp Macadamia nuts (27 g / 1 oz)
2 Medjool dates, pitted (48 g / 1.5 oz)
1/2 lemon, peeled (29 g / 1 oz)
1/2 tsp onion granules (1 g)
1 tsp paprika (2 g)
1/3 tsp chipotle powder (0.8 g)
1/2 jalapeño (with seeds) (15 g / .5 oz)
3/4 cup distilled water (178 g / 6 oz)

Add all ingredients to a blender.
Blend until smooth.

Apple Berry 5-Star Salad
1 large head red leaf lettuce, chopped (360 g / 12 .5 oz)
1.5 cups bok choy, chopped (105 g / 3.7 oz)
1/4 cup dill, chopped (3 g / .1 oz)
1/4 cup leeks, thinly sliced (22 g / .75 oz)
2 stalks celery, chopped (80 g / 2.8 oz)
1 sweet apple, chopped (175 g / 6 oz)
1/2 cup strawberries, sliced (75 g / 2.6 oz)
7 - 10 grape tomatoes, halved (70 g / 2.5 oz)

Add all ingredients to a large salad bowl and mix well.

Dressing: Purple Haze (1 - 2 Servings)
3 Tbsp sesame seeds (27 g / 1 oz)
2 Medjool dates, pitted (48 g / 1.5 oz)
1/2 lemon, peeled (29 g / 1 oz)
1 tsp onion granules (2 g)
1 tsp sage, dried (.3 g)
2 tsp dulce flakes (4 g)
1/8 tsp cayenne pepper
3/4 cup distilled water (178 g / 6 oz)

Add all ingredients to a blender.
Blend until smooth.

Fentastic 5-Star Salad
1/2 large head of iceberg lettuce, chopped (375 g / 13 oz)
4 medium leaves of kale, finely chopped (112 g / 4 oz)
1/4 cup cilantro, chopped (4 g / .1 oz)
1/4 cup red onion, chopped (50 g / 1.75 oz)
1/2 cucumber, sliced (112 g / 4 oz)
2 mandarin oranges (176 g / 6 oz)
1/2 cup red grapes, halved (75 g / 2.6 oz)
1/2 cup yellow bell pepper, chopped
7 - 10 grape tomatoes, halved (70 g / 2.5 oz)

Dressing: Fentastic (1 - 2 Servings)
3 Tbsp pumpkin seeds (23 g / .8 oz)
2 Medjool dates, pitted (48 g / 1.5 oz)
1/2 lemon, peeled (29 g / 1 oz)
1 medium navel orange, peeled (131 g / 4.5 oz)
1 clove garlic (3 g / .1 oz)
1 tsp fennel seed powder (2 g)
3/4 cup distilled water (178 g / 6 oz)

Add all ingredients to a blender.
Blend until smooth.

Southwest Chipotle 5-Star Salad
1 large head of green leaf lettuce, chopped (360 g / 12 .5 oz)
1.5 cups bok choy, chopped (105 g / 3.7 oz)
1/4 cup dill, chopped (3 g / .1 oz)
1/4 cup red onion, chopped (50 g / 1.75 oz)
1/2 cup button mushrooms, sliced (35 g / 1.25 oz)
2 carrots, shredded or chopped (120 g / 4 oz)
1/3 cup raisins (50 g / 1.75 oz)
1/2 cucumber, chopped (112 g / 4 oz)
7 - 10 grape tomatoes, halved (70 g / 2.5 oz)

Add all ingredients to a large salad bowl and mix well.

Dressing: Southwest Chipotle (1 - 2 Servings)
3 Tbsp sunflower seeds (27 g / 1 oz)
2 Medjool dates, pitted (48 g / 1.5 oz)
1/2 lemon, peeled (29 g / 1 oz)
1 tsp onion granules (2 g)
3/4 tsp chipotle powder (1 g)
2 tsp brown mustard (8 g / .3 oz)
3/4 cup distilled water (178 g / 6 oz)

Add all ingredients to a blender.
Blend until smooth.

In A Pickle 5-Star Salad
1 large head of romaine lettuce, chopped (360 g / 12 .5 oz)
1.5 cups napa cabbage, finely chopped (114 g / 4 oz)
1/4 cup cilantro, chopped (4 g / .1 oz)
1/4 cup red onion, chopped (50 g / 1.75 oz)
1 carrot, shredded or chopped (60 g / 2 oz)
1/3 cup raisins (50 g / 1.75 oz)
1 green apple, sliced or chopped (175 g / 6 oz)
7 - 10 grape tomatoes, halved (70 g / 2.5 oz)

Add all ingredients to a large salad bowl and mix well.

Dressing: Pickle Spice (1 - 2 Servings)
3 Tbsp sunflower seeds (27 g / 1 oz)
2 Medjool dates, pitted (48 g / 1.5 oz)
1/2 lemon, peeled (29 g / 1 oz)
1 clove garlic (3 g / .1 oz)
1 tsp pickle spice seasoning (4 g / .1 oz)
3/4 cup distilled water (178 g / 6 oz)

Add all ingredients to a blender.
Blend until smooth.

10

Green Wisdom

"Green juices are the Great Neutralizer."
Dr. Fred Bisci

"There is a real problem with our perception of protein. We must realize that there are quality proteins in greens."
Dr. Fred Bisci

"After you have been eating greens for six months, you will feel that something is missing unless you have them each day."
Dr. Ann Wigmore

"When we learn to eat properly we begin to rebuild our bodies and to fulfill our purpose on this planet to grow in health, creativity, wisdom, and compassion."
Dr. Ann Wigmore

"Green smoothies are the ticket to balance and weight loss."
TannyRaw

"Calories matter and nutrients matter. Health equals how many nutrients per calorie you can pack on every forkful of food. May no calorie go to waste on processed trash."
TannyRaw

"Everything in food works together to create health or disease. The more we think that a single chemical characterizes a whole food, the more we stray into idiocy."
Dr. T. Colin Campbell

"Some people think plant-based diet, whole foods diet is extreme. Half a million people a year will have their chests opened up and a vein taken from their leg and sewn onto their coronary artery. Some people would call that extreme."
Dr. Caldwell Esselstyn Jr.

"Beans and greens are the foods most closely linked in the scientific literature with protection against cancer, diabetes, heart disease, stroke, and dementia."
Dr. Joel Fuhrman

"Eating a high-nutrient diet actually makes you more satisfied with less food, and actually gives the ability to enjoy food more without overeating."
Dr. Joel Fuhrman

"You've got to focus on it until it becomes the easiest thing you do."
TannyRaw

About the Author:
Matt Bennett

Matt Bennett is a Holistic Health Educator with a passionate focus on raw, living foods, and detoxification. Matt has been living a raw vegan lifestyle since 2011, and has experienced the healing of many of his childhood health conditions throughout that time. He now enjoys inspiring people to eat more raw fruits and vegetables with his educational books, recipe ebooks, social media, and a monthly newsletter at myrawintuition.com.

Other Paperback Books By Matt Bennett

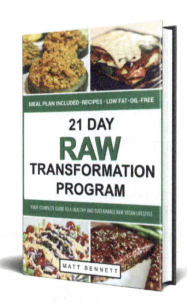 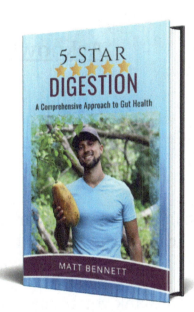

Master the raw vegan diet and your health
with the help of these books!

Available at amazon.com or myrawintuition.com

Additional ebooks, free resources, and our community newsletter are available at myrawintuition.com.

Acknowledgments

Thank you to my editor, Shari Likes Fruit, for your dedication, support, and attention to detail with my work.

And thank you to my family and friends for your support and encouragement in all that I do.

Made in the USA
Coppell, TX
02 October 2023